INSPIRING STORIES OF BOLD, BRAVE,
AND GUTSY WOMEN IN THE U.S. MILITARY

HEROISM

BEGINS WITH

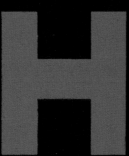

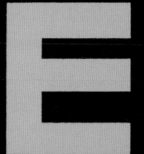

HER

WRITTEN BY **WINIFRED CONKLING** ||| ILLUSTRATED BY **JULIA KUO**

HARPER

An Imprint of HarperCollinsPublishers

Library of Congress Cataloging-in-Publication Data

Names: Conkling, Winifred, author. | Kuo, Julia, author, illustrator.
Title: Heroism begins with her : inspiring stories of bold, brave, and gutsy women in the U.S. Military / Winifred Conkling,
Julia Kuo.
Description: First edition. | New York, NY : Harper, An Imprint of HarperCollinsPublishers, [2019] | Includes bibliographical
references.
Identifiers: LCCN 2018034256 | ISBN 9780062847416 (hardback)
Subjects: LCSH: United States—Armed Forces—Women—Juvenile literature. | Women soldiers—United States—Juvenile
literature. | United States—Armed Forces—Women—Biography—Juvenile literature.
Classification: LCC UB418.W65 C68 2019 | DDC 355.0092/520973—dc23 LC record available at
https://lccn.loc.gov/2018034256

Typography by Catherine San Juan
19 20 21 22 23 SCP 10 9 8 7 6 5 4 3 2 1
❖
First Edition

To the women who serve, with gratitude

CONTENTS

UNEXPECTED PATRIOTS:

WOMEN IN THE REVOLUTIONARY WAR

Women have been involved with the military throughout American history. In every war, from the American Revolution to today's battles in Iraq and Afghanistan, women have proved themselves to be brave, patriotic, honorable, and competent in service to their country.

The positions open to women in the military and the opportunities offered to them have changed dramatically over the years. In the colonial period, it was unthinkable for a woman to enlist in the military. For the first one hundred years of U.S. history, women's lives were much more restricted. They could not own property or sign contracts. If they worked for pay, their wages belonged to their husbands (if they were married) or their fathers (if they were single). Women could not vote. They could not serve on juries or testify in court. And, of course, they could not openly serve in the armed services.

Today, women volunteer for service in all branches of the armed forces: army, navy, air force, marines, and coast guard. And, if qualified, they can serve in any position at any rank or command. For almost 240 years, the military refused to allow women to serve in combat. That last restriction was finally lifted in 2013.

This book tells the inspiring and provocative stories of women who have broken down barriers, defied the odds, and shattered expectations of what female soldiers can be. It includes dozens of examples of female patriotism at its best, from the colonial women who dressed as men so they could serve their country to the modern soldiers who have led military commands and demonstrated their physical and mental toughness both in training and on the battlefield. Women in the military are no longer a novelty; they are an integral and essential part of the American armed forces.

THE REVOLUTIONARY WAR
(1775–1783)

The Revolutionary War was fought between Great Britain and the thirteen colonies, which declared independence and formed the United States of America. Tensions between the colonists and the homeland began to rise with the passage of the Stamp Act in 1765. Colonists resented paying taxes when they were not represented in the British Parliament. Over time, the tensions escalated, finally erupting in the Battles of Lexington and Concord in 1775. The colonists organized the Continental Army on June 14, 1775. After the war, most units of the Continental Army disbanded, and the soldiers and the military women returned to their previous occupations.

WOMEN IN THE REVOLUTIONARY WAR

As far back as the Revolutionary War, women served their country both on the battlefield and behind the scenes. During this time, men in power never considered allowing women to enlist as soldiers in the Continental Army. But some tenacious and deeply patriotic women got around the rules.

A few females decided to see if they could slip through. These women bound their breasts with cloth and dressed in men's clothing. Some were caught immediately, but others got away with the masquerade for months or even years.

While women weren't allowed to pick up arms and fight, they were permitted to play certain support roles for the armed forces. Typically, some of the wives, mothers, and daughters of soldiers followed the military units, cooking, sewing, and washing clothes for the men in exchange for food and a tent to sleep in at night. The army allowed three to six support women per company.

Some people called these women camp followers. General George Washington called them "women of the army." These women were just as tough as the soldiers they served. They had to endure the same hardships and harsh conditions as the men. Some may have been motivated to join the revolution for political reasons, but many others served in the military because they had no other way to support themselves. Women had few opportunities for work

outside the home, leaving them economically dependent on the men in their lives.

In addition to working as camp followers, women also provided nursing care to the military units. The army allowed one matron (supervisor) and ten nurses for every one hundred wounded soldiers. These women were civilians with no military status or benefits, and little or no medical training. Male surgeons and assistants did most of the skilled medical work, and the female nurses did the day-to-day tasks: feeding and bathing patients, cleaning the beds, and emptying chamber pots (since there were no toilets). Nurses were paid two dollars per month; matrons were paid four dollars per month. Not only was the work unpleasant and poorly paid, it was dangerous. Many women became sick while tending their patients.

And we shouldn't discount those women who stayed at home while their husbands served in the Continental Army. These women also did their part keeping the family farms and small businesses running while their husbands were away. Some women even spied and shared the information they learned with the revolutionaries. Other women used their economic power to protest by refusing to buy British-made goods. Women also formed support organizations that raised money and made uniforms for the soldiers.

Some women even performed heroic actions on their own that assisted the Continental Army. For example, on April 26, 1777, in a ride similar to that of the famous Paul Revere, sixteen-year-old Sybil Ludington rode forty miles on horseback to warn the colonists that British troops were burning Danbury, Connecticut.

According to legend, Nancy Hart defended her home in Georgia when six British soldiers went to her cabin and asked if she had seen a man they were tracking. She said she had not seen him—even though she had—and then the men killed her prized turkey and demanded that she cook it for them. She did as she was told and fed the men and served them wine. While the soldiers were eating, Hart and her daughter stole the soldiers' weapons, leaving them drunk and defenseless by the end of the meal. She held the men hostage, and when her husband and other neighbors arrived, they hanged the men. While historians have found it difficult to separate fact from folklore, there is archaeological evidence to back up the story: in 1912 when a group of construction workers leveled the land near the Hart farm to put in a railroad, they unearthed a row of six skeletons that had been buried for more than a century.

While most historians focus their attention on the men who led the American Revolution, the important role of women in the military should not be overlooked. The women who served in combat may not have been great in number, but their contributions were significant. Against the odds, they took up arms and became the first group of American women to fight for their country.

ESTABLISHING THE ARMED FORCES

One of the first actions of the Continental Congress was to establish a network of national defense. In the United States, the armed forces are divided into five branches, all under the command of the president of the United States.

- **Army** (founded June 14, 1775): Soldiers dedicated to land-based operations.
- **Navy** (founded October 13, 1775): Sailors dedicated to defending the United States at sea and securing the oceans around the world.
- **Marines** (founded November 10, 1775): Soldiers in a rapid-reaction force, fighting on land and sea. The marines were initially a ground force within the navy but were separated into an independent branch of the military in 1798.
- **Coast Guard** (founded August 4, 1790): Dedicated to protecting domestic waterways by performing rescues, enforcing laws, and keeping waterways clear.
- **Air Force** (founded September 18, 1947): Dedicated to protecting American interests overseas, with the focus on air power.

MARGARET CORBIN:
READY! AIM! FIRE!

MARGARET CORBIN

Margaret Cochran Corbin didn't intend to become a soldier, but when the situation presented itself, she wasn't willing to accept her husband's death without a fight.

Margaret was born in western Pennsylvania on November 12, 1751. She was orphaned at age five when her father was killed and her mother was kidnapped during a battle with a group of Native Americans. Margaret lived with an uncle until age twenty-one when she married John Corbin, a Virginia farmer. During the Revolutionary War, John enlisted in the cannon crew of First Company of the Pennsylvania Artillery. When he was called into battle, Margaret decided to go with him.

As a nurse, Margaret tended the soldiers injured in battle. She also brought water to the fighting men and to her husband, who used it to wipe down the cannons between each shot he fired to prevent the gunpowder residue from igniting. On November 16, 1776, Margaret and John fought in a battle to defend Fort Washington in northern Manhattan. The odds were against them: there were 600 American soldiers and more than 4,000 British.

Under enemy fire, twenty-five-year-old Margaret watched her husband clean, load, and fire his cannon again and again and again. During the fighting, John was struck in the head by enemy fire, and he dropped to the ground next to his cannon. Margaret rushed to him, but he was already dead.

Instead of giving up and accepting defeat, Margaret quickly went to work. The enemy was still firing on them! Although she had never fired a cannon before, she repeated the steps she had seen her husband do a hundred times before: she swabbed out the hot gun barrel with water to remove any unexploded gunpowder, picked up the ramming staff and loaded a cannonball, then fired.

Margaret proved to be an excellent shot. Her aim was true and she was able to quickly fire and reload. She stayed and valiantly fought at her husband's post until she, too, suffered enemy fire. She was hit in the arm, chest, and jaw.

After the Battle of Fort Washington, Margaret went to Philadelphia to recover. She lost the use of her left arm and was disfigured by her injuries. To compensate her for her disability, the Executive Council of Pennsylvania gave her $30—an amount equal to about $500 today—and passed the case to the Board of War. On July 6, 1779, the Continental Congress passed a resolution that read:

> Resolved, That Margaret Corbin, who was wounded and disabled in the attack on Fort Washington, whilst she heroically filled the post of her husband who was killed by her side serving a piece of artillery, do receive, during her natural life, or the continuance of said disability, one-half of the monthly pay drawn by a soldier in service of these states; and that she now receive out of the public stores, one suit of cloaths, or value thereof in money.

With that action, Margaret became the first woman in the United States to receive a military pension from Congress.

Margaret Corbin died in Highland Falls, New York, on January 16, 1800, at age forty-eight. Her military service was all but forgotten until 1926, when the New York State Chapter of the Daughters of the American Revolution identified her grave. The group had Margaret's body removed from the grave so that a doctor could confirm her identity by examining her skeleton, which showed damage to the face, chest, and shoulder. She was reburied with full military honors at the cemetery of the United States Military Academy at West Point. She is one of two Revolutionary War soldiers buried there.

WHO WAS MOLLY PITCHER?

Some historians believe that Margaret Corbin may have inspired the iconic figure "Molly Pitcher," the woman who brought water to thirsty soldiers on the battlefields during the Revolutionary War. Others claim that the story of Molly Pitcher may have been a tribute to Mary Ludwig Hays McCauley, a woman who followed her husband into battle and picked up his weapon when he was injured in the Battle of Monmouth in 1778. It is also possible that Molly Pitcher was not meant to honor the achievements of any single woman but instead to recognize the contributions of the many women who supported the soldiers during the Revolutionary War.

This 1876 lithograph by Nathaniel Currier and James Merritt Ives shows an image of "Molly Pitcher." While the last name "Pitcher" became popular, the women almost certainly carried the water in pails rather than pitchers.

DEBORAH SAMPSON GANNETT:
A SOLDIER'S SECRET

DEBORAH
SAMPSON GANNETT

Deborah Sampson was neither the first nor the only woman to dress as a man and fight as a soldier during the American Revolution, but she is the most famous. Her story is remembered because after the war she wrote about her experiences disguising herself as a man in order to serve in the Continental Army.

Deborah was born on December 17, 1760, in Plympton, Massachusetts. When she was five years old, her father abandoned the family, leaving behind his wife and seven children. Her mother struggled to support the family, and when Deborah was ten years old she became an indentured servant, meaning she was hired out to work to earn her room and board. She lived with the Thomas family in Middleborough, Massachusetts, and worked on their farm.

While there, Deborah learned to read and write from other members of the family. When she turned eighteen, she was free to start a life of her own. She became a spinner and weaver, and she taught school for several summers. In the winter of 1781, the Continental Congress put out a call for soldiers, and Deborah decided to enlist. While most of the fighting of the Revolutionary War was over, some soldiers were still needed as peace was being negotiated.

On December 17, 1781, Deborah's twenty-first birthday, she dressed as a man and went to

After her service, Deborah Sampson Gannett became the first American woman to go on a lecture tour about being a woman in the Continental Army and masquerading as Robert Shurtliff.

the local army recruiting office. She told the recruiter that her name was Timothy Thayer, and she took the cash payment for enlisting in the military. That night, still dressed as Timothy, Deborah went to a local tavern. No one recognized her.

But when it was time to report for duty, Timothy Thayer didn't show up. A woman who had watched Deborah sign the recruitment papers had noticed that "Timothy" held a pen in the same unusual way as Deborah, who had an injured forefinger. When the recruiters questioned Deborah about her identity, she confessed to her fraud and returned the money, except the cash she had used to buy a new dress.

But Deborah didn't give up. A few months later, she enlisted again, this time in a community where no one knew her. While historians debate the exact dates, most believe that on May 23, 1782, Deborah Sampson signed up for a three-year term with the Fourth Massachusetts Regiment using the name Robert Shurtliff (also spelled Shirtliffe and Shurtleff). To pass as a man, she bound her breasts with a cloth and wore loose-fitting shirts. She was five feet, eight inches tall, quite tall since women of the time averaged only about five feet in height. While she didn't have a beard, neither did most of the teenage boys who were accepted into the ranks of the Continental Army.

As a soldier, Deborah learned to charge with a bayonet and fire her musket twice in one minute. She was chosen for the light infantry division, which included younger, more athletic soldiers. On her first assignment in June 1782, Deborah encountered a soldier from her hometown—a former neighbor. But he didn't recognize her, so her identity remained a secret.

She had another close call when loyalists attacked her while on patrol. Deborah was charged with a bayonet and shot in the leg. She begged her fellow soldiers to let her die. Instead, they took her to a field hospital where the doctor treated a wound on the left side of her head. She was afraid to tell him about the injury to her thigh because the doctor would cut away her pants and discover that she was a woman. To keep her secret safe, after she left the hospital, Deborah used a penknife and a sewing needle to remove one of two musket balls from her leg. She couldn't reach the second one, so it remained in her leg the rest of her life.

Deborah served for a year and a half before anyone found out she was a woman. Her identity was finally revealed in 1783 when she came down with a serious fever while camped near Philadelphia. She was taken to a hospital and examined by Dr. Barnabas Binney, who discovered the truth. He sympathized with Deborah and took her to his home so that she could recover away from the other soldiers. When she was healthy, she returned to her unit as Robert Shurtliff.

The doctor told General John Patterson, the commander of West Point, about Deborah's true identity. Although Deborah was not punished, she was not allowed to continue to serve. Deborah (Robert Shurtliff) was honorably discharged from the army on October 25, 1783.

After her military service, Deborah married Benjamin Gannett and gave birth to three children and adopted a fourth. Her husband was a farmer, but they didn't have much money. In 1792, Deborah petitioned the Commonwealth of Massachusetts to collect the back pay she was owed from her service as a soldier. She also spent years campaigning for veterans' benefits she felt entitled to receive.

Patriot Paul Revere learned about Deborah's petition for financial assistance, and on February 20, 1804, he wrote a letter to the government on her behalf. "She did a Soldier's duty; and that while in the Army, She was wounded," Revere wrote. "I have no doubt your humanity will prompt you to do all in Your power to get her some relief." After Revere sent his letter, Deborah was awarded a pension of $4 per month, starting in 1805.

In 1797, Deborah wrote *The Female Review; or, Memoirs of an American Young Lady*. She also prepared a lecture titled "The American Heroine" about her time in the military. During the presentation she dressed in uniform, marched, demonstrated how to drill with her musket, and answered questions about her life as Robert Shurtliff.

Deborah Sampson Gannett died of yellow fever on April 29, 1827, at age sixty-six.

PRUDENCE CUMMINGS WRIGHT:
THE WOMEN'S MILITIA

PRUDENCE
CUMMINGS WRIGHT

In the 1770s, the women of Pepperell, Massachusetts, were serious patriots. After learning about the Boston Tea Party, they gathered on the town green and burned their imported tea. When the men in town were ordered to Boston to fight in the Revolutionary War, the women organized their own militia to protect the town. Prudence Cummings Wright, a thirty-five-year-old mother of six, commanded an informal militia, which she called Mrs. David Wright's Guard.

For Prudence, the Revolutionary War was personal. She was born on November 26, 1740, in Hollis, New Hampshire, where her father served as town clerk. Prudence's father supported independence, but many other family members—including two of her three brothers—were loyalists, who supported the British.

In 1761, Prudence married David Wright, a patriot and a member of the local militia. She gave birth to eleven children between 1763 and 1783, and she wanted her children to grow up in a free and independent nation.

In April 1775, the women in Pepperell learned that loyalist spies were planning to smuggle important information from Canada to Boston. In order to complete their journey, the men would have to pass through Pepperell and cross the Nashua River at Jewett's bridge. Prudence learned that one of the spies was rumored to be her brother Thomas.

Prudence felt more loyalty to her country than to her brother. She recruited thirty or forty women and encouraged them to dress in their husbands' old clothes. On the night the spies were expected to arrive in Pepperell, the women carried muskets, pitchforks, and anything else they could use as weapons and gathered by the bridge to wait for the spies.

That night, Captain Leonard Whiting of Hollis was stopped on the bridge. The women searched him and found "treasonable correspondence" hidden in his boots. He was held prisoner at a Pepperell tavern overnight and then moved to Groton, where he was taken into official custody.

According to Wright family legend, a second man—Prudence's brother Thomas—had been with Whiting, but he turned back when he saw his sister waiting for him on the bridge. Other accounts have Thomas Wright run out of town, never to return.

On March 19, 1777, two years after the event, Pepperell town officials voted to award Wright and the other women a payment of seven pounds, seventeen shillings, and sixpence for their services during the Revolutionary War—an amount equal to about $1,200 in today's money.

Prudence Wright died on December 2, 1824. She is the only woman known to have served as a militia leader during the Revolutionary War.

This 1940 photograph shows the Nehemiah Jewett bridge in Pepperell, Massachusetts, the site where Prudence Wright and her fellow "Minutewomen" captured Leonard Whiting on his way to deliver documents to the British.

DON'T MESS WITH TEXAS:

WOMEN IN THE MEXICAN-AMERICAN WAR

After the Revolutionary War, most soldiers were sent home. Only two regiments remained active, and in 1796 these units became the core of the newly formed United States Army. These soldiers were no longer revolutionaries; their new mission was to defend and protect their new country, the United States of America.

From its earliest days, the army was kept busy. The military faced frequent battles with various Native American tribes, as well as another war against Britain in 1812. As the nation expanded west, so did conflict about who would control that frontier land. Native Americans owned the land, but the Americans wanted it, too.

One of the key issues involved the sovereignty of Texas, which had once been part of Mexico but had declared its independence in a revolution fought from 1835 to 1836. A decade later, in 1845, Texas agreed to join the United States and become the twenty-eighth state.

But Mexico didn't agree to the arrangement, warning that making Texas a part of the United States would lead to war. And it did. In the Mexican-American War the army invaded and seized the land that now makes up the southwestern part of the country, including parts of the current states of New Mexico, Arizona, Utah, and California. In a final peace agreement, the United States took possession of the western land and paid Mexico $15 million as part of the Treaty of Guadalupe Hidalgo.

Once again, women refused to sit on the sidelines. During the Mexican-American War, females still could not openly serve as soldiers, but many determined women found a way to be involved, just as they had during the American Revolutionary War. Hundreds again followed the troops and supported them by cooking, sewing, and laundering their clothes. These women were given one food ration per day by the military, plus the soldiers paid them for each item of clothing they washed.

Many of the women who stayed at home supported the troops by organizing dinners, dances, and parades for the soldiers. On a more practical level, they kept family businesses and households running while the men were at war, which kept society functioning so that men had their jobs and families to return to in peacetime.

Not all Americans supported the Mexican-American War. Abolitionists—women and men

THE MEXICAN-AMERICAN WAR (1846–1848)

The Mexican-American War was fought between the United States and Mexico following the American annexation of the Republic of Texas, which had declared independence from Mexico in 1836. Mexico still considered Texas a Mexican territory. This period of westward expansion brought debate about the spread of slavery, an issue that would be addressed in the American Civil War in the 1860s.

who opposed slavery—feared slavery would expand into the western territories. The western lands almost doubled the size of the United States, and if slavery was allowed in the new states, then proslavery forces would have greater representation in Congress.

Slavery wasn't the main concern for other Americans who supported westward expansion. Neither was the fact that Native Americans owned much of the land during this expansion. Jane McManus Cazneau was a journalist for the *New-York Tribune*, the New York *Sun*, and the *Democratic Review*. She supported the idea of Manifest Destiny, the concept that the United States had the right and responsibility to extend its reach from coast to coast. In addition to writing her opinions, Cazneau became the first female war correspondent in U.S. history.

As a result of the Mexican-American War, the United States acquired vast amounts of land in the west. The slavery issue remained a source of tension, ultimately setting the stage for the American Civil War thirteen years later.

Jane McManus Cazneau (1807–1878), a war correspondent and unofficial diplomat to Mexico, also used the name Cora Montgomery.

SARAH BOWMAN BORGINNES:
AN HONORARY COLONEL

SARAH BOWMAN
BORGINNES

Sarah Bowman Borginnes was cool under fire. During the siege of Fort Texas, she served as both soldier and cook, alternating between firing cannons at the enemy and preparing hot meals for her fellow soldiers.

The details of Sarah's birth are uncertain: she was born in either Missouri or Tennessee in either 1812 or 1813. She was illiterate—she signed her name with an X on census forms—but she spoke Spanish fluently. She was more than six feet tall, physically strong, and intimidating. A Texas Ranger said, "She could whip any man, fair fight or foul, could shoot a pistol better than anyone in the region and at black-jack could outplay (or out cheat) the slickest professional gambler."

When it became clear that Mexico was going to resist the annexation of Texas in 1845, General Zachary Taylor began to recruit soldiers. When Sarah's husband enlisted in the Eighth Infantry at Jefferson Barracks Military Post in Missouri, Sarah signed on as a cook.

Her first husband became sick and left the military, but Sarah remarried a man named Borginnes (also spelled Borginnis, Boginnis, and Bourget, among other variations) and she continued to follow the troops. She served as principal cook at Fort Texas (later renamed Fort Brown). In May 1846, the fort was under siege; for six days the troops were under constant overwhelming attack. Sarah was given a musket and joined in the fighting.

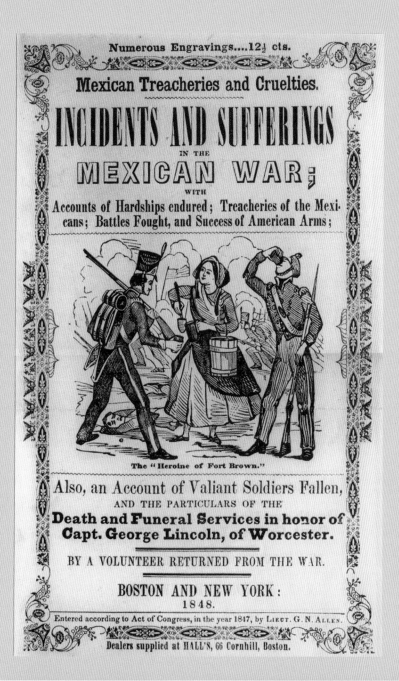

This line drawing depicts Sarah Borginnes (1812–1866) as the "Heroine of Fort Brown." It was used in the promotion of the book *Incidents and Sufferings in the Mexican War.*

She also continued to provide hot meals three times a day, and she tended the wounded. It was said that she carried buckets filled with coffee to the troops manning the guns, even though bullets hit her bonnet and bread tray. Eventually the Mexican soldiers were forced to retreat. Her efforts earned her the name "Heroine of Fort Brown."

Sarah also participated in the Battle of Buena Vista, where she reloaded weapons, nursed the wounded, and fired a cannon. When she found out that her friend Captain George Lincoln had been killed, she recovered his body so that it would not be disrespected or looted.

After the war, Sarah moved to El Paso and opened a hotel, which proved to be a popular spot among travelers during the 1849 gold rush. She later moved to Arizona and ran a saloon. Sarah had several husbands and adopted a number of Mexican and Native American children. She died from a spider bite on December 22, 1866, and was buried at Fort Yuma with full military honors. (When Fort Yuma was decommissioned in 1890, her body was removed and reburied at San Francisco National Cemetery in a grave marked Sarah Bowman.)

Following her death, General Zachary Taylor brevetted her to colonel, meaning she was given the honorary title, without the authority or benefits associated with being an officer of that rank. With her posthumous promotion, Sarah Bowman Borginnes became the first female colonel of the United States Army.

ELIZABETH CAROLINE NEWCOM:
THE THINGS WE DO FOR LOVE

In September 1847, Elizabeth Caroline Newcom (also spelled Newcum, Newcume, and Newcome) dressed as a man and enlisted in Company D of the Missouri Volunteer Infantry at Fort Leavenworth, Kansas, using the name Bill Newcom. The twenty-two-year-old joined the military so that she could follow her boyfriend, First Lieutenant Amandus V. Schnabel, from St. Louis.

With very little, if any, training, Elizabeth and the other enlisted soldiers marched along the Santa Fe Trail to Fort Mann, near present-day Dodge City, Kansas. In May 1848, Elizabeth decided to leave the military, perhaps because she was pregnant. Her boyfriend encouraged her to escape on a supply wagon heading east. She tried to get away, but another soldier caught her and revealed her identity. She was discharged from the military after ten months of service.

ELIZABETH CAROLINE
NEWCOM

In July 1848, she applied for a land grant that had been promised to soldiers who fought in the Mexican-American War. Congress approved her request: Elizabeth Newcom was granted 160 acres as well as the pay equal to that of a soldier in battle for ten months.

Elizabeth and her boyfriend were never reunited. She married John Smith in 1853. Little is known about the fate of the baby or how Elizabeth spent the rest of her life.

WOMEN WARRIORS:

WOMEN IN THE CIVIL WAR

The Civil War divided and devastated the nation. An astonishing 620,000 people died—one out of every four soldiers who served—and another 476,000 were wounded during the four years of intense fighting.

No one could escape the impact of the war. In this conflict, women played an essential part both on and off the battlefield. Once again, women supported the troops by serving as cooks and laundry workers, but during this war females had more formal opportunities to serve as nurses and medical assistants for both the Union (Northern) and Confederate (Southern) forces.

At the beginning of the war, women in the North organized the Women's Central Association of Relief. The association pressured the Union army to establish the Sanitary Commission, the first official agency dedicated to setting and enforcing sanitation and health regulations in the army. Through the Sanitary Commission, women were able to improve patient care by distributing supplies and establishing good medical practices. The nurses were volunteers without military rank or status, but they were more professional now and able to provide a higher standard of

THE AMERICAN CIVIL WAR (1861–1865)

The American Civil War was fought between the Union forces in the North and the Confederate forces in the South. While many factors contributed to the war, the key issues were slavery and states' rights. More specifically, the free northern and the Southern slave states differed in their opinions about whether the federal government had the right to prohibit slavery in the western territories. The fighting began when Confederates attacked Fort Sumter on April 12, 1861, in South Carolina and ended with General Robert E. Lee's surrender on April 9, 1865, in Virginia.

care. In addition to changing bandages and cleaning wounds, some nurses were called on to assist with surgeries, including amputations. An estimated 3,000 women volunteered as nurses during the Civil War.

Women could not openly serve in the armed forces, but that didn't stop them from trying to sneak in. Historians estimate that at least 400 women—and possibly as many as 750—dressed as men and served

Clara Barton

CLARA BARTON AND THE RED CROSS

Clara Barton (1821–1912) was one nurse who helped reform medical care during the Civil War. Barton first learned about nursing when at age ten she helped care for her older brother after he fell from the roof of a barn and was severely injured. She did not attend nursing school. Instead, she learned how to care for the sick and injured through firsthand experience during the Civil War. At her own expense, she provided medical supplies to the Union army. She also tended the injured on the battlefield and in hospitals. She helped both Union and Confederate soldiers. She went on to organize the American Red Cross and serve as its first president. Despite her contributions, she was never recognized by the military.

in both the Union and Confederate armies. Some women enlisted for the money: at the time a maid in New York earned $4 to $7 a month, while a Union soldier collected $13 a month. Others were motivated by ideals: they either fought to end slavery or to defend the practice as the economic backbone of the Southern economy. In either case, these women willingly enlisted and risked their lives for their beliefs.

At first, male soldiers didn't realize that women were fighting in their ranks. That changed in July 1863, on Cemetery Ridge near Gettysburg, Pennsylvania, when Union soldiers gathered to bury hundreds of dead bodies after battle. Among the dead were the remains of an unidentified young woman who was wearing the uniform of a Confederate private. The men had to face the truth: women were fighting, too. In the heat of battle, the relevant issue was not whether a soldier was male or female; it was whether a soldier fought for the Union or Confederacy. Over time, the hardened soldiers worried less about the possibility of hurting a woman in battle. When fighting near Texas in May 1864, Sergeant Robert Ardry of the Eleventh Illinois Infantry encountered several Confederate women soldiers. "They fought like demons," Ardry wrote in a letter to his father, "and we cut them down like dogs."

It was easier during the Civil War than in previous conflicts for women to enlist and fight because the armies employed more "citizen soldiers" with no military training. Both Union and Confederate forces were so eager for volunteers that they often skipped the entrance physicals. At the time, soldiers typically slept in their uniforms and bathed alone or not at all. Uniforms were heavy and loose fitting, so women could hide their bodies behind bulky clothes. A woman's lack of facial hair was not always a clear indication of sex because the military enlisted very young men and boys, some only twelve years old.

The women who stayed at home also had to deal with wartime challenges. When the men in the family went off to fight, the women managed their households, farms, and businesses. In addition to a heavy load of physical labor, many women sewed uniforms for their soldiers; others gathered food, medical supplies, and bedding for military posts and hospitals.

After the war, more than 2 percent of the nation's population had died and nearly the same number had been injured. Many women were forced to continue to handle traditionally male responsibilities even after the fighting ended.

Not much is known about Frances Clayton (ca. 1830–1865 or later), except that in 1865 she dressed as both a woman and a male soldier. This photograph provides evidence of women dressing as men to serve in the military during the Civil War.

DOROTHEA LYNDE DIX:
FOUNDER OF THE FIRST FEMALE NURSING CORPS

DOROTHEA LYNDE DIX

Before the Civil War, nursing was a male profession. While women had followed the troops and tended the wounded in battles, they did not do so as official, trained nurses. Reformer Dorothea Lynde Dix changed that.

Dix was born in Hampden, Maine, on April 4, 1802. As the oldest of three children, she took care of her younger brothers because her mother suffered from depression and her father was an alcoholic who was often abusive. When she was twelve years old, Dix went to live with her grandmother and then with an aunt in Worcester, Massachusetts. She learned to read and write and began teaching at age fourteen. In addition to teaching well-to-do children in a well-equipped school in Boston, she also taught poor children out of a makeshift

During her career, Dorothea Dix founded more than thirty hospitals for the mentally ill across the United States. She also established the first nursing corps for the United States Army.

school in the barn at her grandmother's house.

Dix's life changed in 1841 when she began teaching Sunday school at East Cambridge Jail, a women's prison. She was appalled at the harsh and unsanitary conditions inside the facility. At the time, people who were mentally ill were often caged or chained in unheated cells with little or no clothing. Inspired by a group of reformers she had met during a trip to England several years earlier, Dix began to work on behalf of the mentally ill. She documented the cruel and abusive treatment of inmates in both prisons and mental asylums and lobbied for governmental reform of prisons and improved care for the mentally ill.

When the Civil War began in 1861, Dix volunteered to help. Two months after the war started, Secretary of War Simon Cameron accepted her offer and appointed fifty-nine-year-old Dix as superintendent of women nurses for the Union army. He knew that Dix was compassionate, and he admired her efforts toward prison reform. While not a military position—she had no official rank—Dix became the first woman to serve in an important role in the federal government.

In her new position, Dix organized the 3,000 women who served as nurses during the Civil War. At the time, there were only 150 hospitals in the country, and there were no formal nursing schools. Dix didn't let the lack of infrastructure stop her from helping those in need. She set up field hospitals, managed supplies, and recruited and trained the nurses. She established guidelines for the profession: nurses were to be thirty to fifty years old and plain looking, they were to wear black or brown dresses—no hoop skirts—and they could not wear jewelry or makeup. Dix worried that male doctors and patients would victimize or exploit the nurses if they were attractive.

Dix—sometimes called Dragon Dix because of her firmness and inflexibility—was feared by nurses and not well liked by army doctors. She often quarreled with physicians over control of the hospitals and the hiring and firing of nurses; many doctors didn't want to work with female nurses. The issue was resolved—but not to Dix's satisfaction—in October 1863 when the War Department gave authority to the doctors to assign hospital staff.

Dix worked without pay, as did the nurses under her care, even though male nurses were paid $20.50 a month. Dix knew this wasn't right, and she lobbied for wages for her female nurses. They were eventually paid 40 cents a day for their work. Despite the frustrations, Dix did not resign from her post until August 1865 at the end of the war. She did not take off a single day in four years of service.

Rather than retire from public service, Dix returned to her work on behalf of the disabled, prisoners, and mentally ill. By 1881, she was an invalid and moved into the New Jersey State Hospital, which she had helped build years before. She died at age eighty-five on July 17, 1887, and was buried in Mount Auburn Cemetery in Cambridge, Massachusetts.

WELL-KNOWN WRITERS WHO SERVED

Women from all walks of life volunteered to serve as nurses during the Civil War. Several female authors served as nurses, including Jane Stuart Woolsey, who wrote *Hospital Days: Reminiscences of a Civil War Nurse* in 1868, and Katherine Prescott Wormeley, an editor and translator of French literature.

One of the most famous nurse volunteers was Louisa May Alcott, a poet and novelist who wrote for the *Atlantic Monthly*. After the war, Alcott wrote *Little Women* (1868) and *Little Men* (1871), among other bestselling books. Alcott wrote about her experience as a volunteer nurse during the Battle of Fredericksburg in her 1863 book *Hospital Sketches*.

Louisa May Alcott (1832–1888)

SARAH EMMA EDMONDS:
MASTER OF DISGUISE

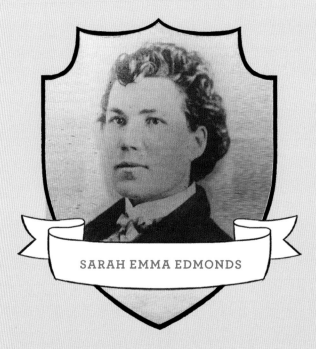

SARAH EMMA EDMONDS

Sarah Emma Edmonds was a master of disguise. Like a number of other women, she dressed as a man in order to enlist in the military, but she took her masquerade one step further and assumed other identities while working as a spy for the Union army.

Sarah was born in December 1841 in New Brunswick, Canada. When she was fifteen years old, she ran away to escape her father's plan to marry her off to one of his creditors. She fled to a small town in Canada and changed her last name from Edmondson to Edmonds. She lived there for about a year but moved again, this time to the United States, and disguised herself as a man.

Sarah took the name Franklin Flint Thompson and found a job as a traveling Bible salesman based in Hartford, Connecticut. She would not have been able to work and live as a woman alone, but by assuming a male identity she could. "I could only thank God that I was free and could go forward and work, and was not obliged to stay home and weep," she said.

Sarah may have been inspired by a book she read as a girl, *Fanny Campbell, the Female Pirate Captain* by Maturin Murray Ballou, which told the story of a woman who dressed as a man so that she could have adventures as a pirate on the high seas.

When the Civil War started in 1861, Sarah heard President Abraham Lincoln's call for volunteers for the war effort. She wanted to support her adopted country, so on May 25, 1861, she dressed as a man and enlisted for a three-year term in Company F of the Second Michigan Infantry, known as the Flint Union Greys. She continued to use the name Franklin Thompson.

According to her 1864 autobiography *Nurse and Spy in the Union Army: The Adventures, Experiences of a Woman in Hospitals, Camps, and Battle-Fields,* Sarah volunteered to work as a spy. In the book, she claims she used many disguises to allow her to travel behind enemy lines and collect information. She then shared this intelligence with officers in the North.

At one point, Sarah assumed the identity of a black man by wearing a black wig and using silver nitrate to color her skin. In another situation she imitated an Irish brogue and pretended to be a peddler who sold apples and soap to Confederate soldiers. In one of her most successful campaigns, Sarah again dyed her skin and took on the identity of an African American laundry worker. As part of her job, she dug through the pockets of officers' pants and jackets. When washing one officer's jacket, she found some official papers and smuggled them back to the Union officers.

Sarah's military career ended when she developed malaria. She knew that her gender would be revealed if she went to a military doctor, so she checked herself into a private hospital instead. She intended to return to her regiment when she recovered, but she saw

a poster that listed Frank Thompson—her male identity—as a deserter. She could face execution for desertion if she returned to the military, so she abandoned her male identity and began to live as Sarah Edmonds again.

Sarah got a job with the United States Christian Commission as a nurse in a Washington, DC, hospital. A few years later, she published her autobiography, which sold more than 175,000 copies. Sarah donated the money she made to organizations dedicated to helping veterans.

In 1867, Sarah married Linus H. Seelye, a childhood friend. They had three children, all of whom died before reaching adulthood, so they adopted two boys.

Sarah worked for eight years to receive credit for her military service and to be cleared of the charge of desertion. The charges were finally dropped and she began to receive a military pension of $12 a month starting in 1886. In 1897, she became the only woman admitted to the Grand Army of the Republic, a veterans' organization for soldiers who fought for the Union during the Civil War. She died on September 5, 1898, and was buried in La Porte, Texas. Three years later she was reburied with military honors in the Grand Army of the Republic section of Washington Cemetery in Houston.

JENNIE HODGERS:
BECOMING ALBERT CASHIER

Albert Cashier was born Jennie Hodgers. When she was nineteen years old, she assumed the identity of Albert Cashier to enlist in the military, but unlike other female soldiers who dressed as men to join the armed forces, Jennie chose to live as a man for the rest of her life.

Jennie was born on December 25, 1843, in Clogherhead, Ireland. The details of her early life have been lost, but some reports indicate that her stepfather asked her to dress as a boy so that she could get a job. As a young adult, she came to the United States and made her way to Belvidere, Illinois.

ALBERT CASHIER

It is not known if Jennie felt more comfortable living as a male or if she changed her identity for economic reasons. She could make $13 a month as a soldier, more than twice what she could have earned if she had applied for work as a female. She couldn't read or write—she signed her name with an *X*—and she almost certainly would have suffered from poverty if she had lived as a woman.

Whatever her motivation, on August 6, 1862, she enlisted in the Ninety-Fifth Illinois Infantry as Albert Cashier. At five feet tall and 110 pounds, Albert was the smallest soldier in the regiment. But despite his size, Albert fought in more than forty battles. In May 1863, Confederate soldiers captured Albert; he escaped after wresting a gun away from one of his captors.

Albert served the full three-year enlistment and was discharged on August 17, 1865. He settled in Saunemin, Illinois, where he continued to live as a man. He held a number of jobs, including farmworker and cemetery worker. Albert enjoyed other benefits of a male identity: he collected a military pension and voted in elections (even though women did not have the right to vote until 1920).

Albert kept his gender a secret until November 1910 when he was hit by a car. The doctors in the hospital kept the secret and arranged to have him recover at the Soldiers and Sailors Home in Quincy, Illinois. Albert developed dementia in March 1913 and was sent to the Watertown State Hospital for the insane.

The hospital proved to be a complete disaster. The doctors learned that Albert was female and forced him to wear dresses. The newspapers heard about the story and published articles about Albert. A reporter from the *Hartford Republican* wrote:

> *I had expected to meet an amazon. A woman who had fought in the death grapple of a nation and had lived and toiled as a man through half a century should be big, strong, and masculine. And when I entered her hospital ward there rose and came to meet me, in her faded soldier's uniform, just a little, frail, sweet-faced, old-lady, who might be anybody's grandmother.*

When it was discovered that Albert was female, he lost his military pension and the government charged him with fraud. Fellow soldiers from the Ninety-Fifth Illinois testified that Albert had fought with bravery and valor on dangerous missions and was entitled to a pension. Their efforts persuaded the government to reestablish his status as a veteran.

Albert Cashier died on October 10, 1915, and was buried, dressed for eternity as a man in a full military uniform. His tombstone listed his name as Albert Cashier. More than fifty years later, a second grave marker was placed next to the first one, and read "Albert Cashier born Jennie Hodgers."

SUSIE KING TAYLOR:
THE FIRST AFRICAN AMERICAN NURSE

During the Civil War, Susie King Taylor became the first African American woman to serve as an army nurse. She enlisted in the First South Carolina Volunteers, an all-black army troop, later renamed the Thirty-Third United States Colored Infantry Regiment.

Susan Ann Baker was born enslaved at a plantation in Liberty County, Georgia, on August 6, 1848. She was the oldest of nine children. With her owner's permission when she was seven years old, she and her younger brother moved to Savannah to live with their grandmother. While there, she attended an illegal school run by a free black woman and learned to read and write.

SUSIE KING TAYLOR

When she was in her teens, Susie was arrested at a suburban church for singing freedom hymns. She was sent back to her mother's house on the plantation. The Civil War started soon after, and in April 1862 Susie moved to St. Simons Island, Georgia, which was occupied by Union forces. When the soldiers learned that she was able to read and write, they provided her with the resources to continue teaching. She taught children during the day and adults at night, becoming the first black teacher for freed African American students in Georgia.

Susie married Edward King, a noncommissioned officer with the First South Carolina Volunteers.

Susie King Taylor volunteered as a nurse with her husband's military regiment during the Civil War. Like most female nurses—both black and white—she was never paid for her service or recognized as an official member of the military.

After the war, she and her husband returned to Savannah, where she started a school for freed children. Edward died in an accident at the pier where he worked unloading ships.

In 1879, Susie married Russell Taylor. In 1902, Susie wrote *Reminiscences of My Life in Camp with the 33d United States Colored Troops, Late 1st S.C. Volunteers*, becoming the only African American woman to publish a memoir of her experiences during the Civil War. Susie King Taylor died on October 6, 1912.

AFRICAN AMERICANS IN THE MILITARY

African Americans have served in the military throughout U.S. history. During the Revolutionary War, an estimated 5,000 African American soldiers served in the military, and 20,000 more joined the British army. (The British had more recruits because they offered black slaves their freedom if they enlisted.) The loyalist recruits formed the Black Pioneers, the only black regiment to participate in the war. (They didn't fight; they were engineers and construction workers.)

After the revolution, African Americans had limited opportunities to serve in the military. That changed during the Civil War when almost 180,000 African Americans served in the Union army and more than 19,000 joined the Union navy. On the Confederate side, blacks were used for labor rather than combat because slave owners in the South were afraid of giving arms to African American soldiers. At least 40,000 African Americans died during the Civil War, most from infection and disease.

Blacks served in segregated units, typically led by white officers. In 1863, the government set up the Bureau of Colored Troops to manage the large number of African American recruits. At the insistence of President Abraham Lincoln, African American soldiers received pay, rations, supplies, and medical care equal to that provided to white soldiers.

For the next hundred years, the military remained segregated. Black and white soldiers could not serve side by side until after World War II, when President Harry S. Truman signed an executive order integrating the armed services.

HARRIET TUBMAN:
BEYOND THE UNDERGROUND RAILROAD

HARRIET TUBMAN

Harriet Tubman is best known for her courageous work as a conductor on the Underground Railroad, repeatedly putting her life at risk to help other enslaved people find freedom. But her work on behalf of freedom did not end there. During the Civil War, Tubman set up a spy ring, led an attack against plantation owners, and launched a campaign that freed an astonishing 750 enslaved people in South Carolina.

Sometime around 1822, Araminta "Minty" Ross was born into slavery on a farm on Maryland's Eastern Shore. She learned the harsh realities of slavery from an early age: when she was twelve years old, her master threw a heavy iron weight in the direction of a slave he thought was trying to run away. The man's aim was off and the iron smashed into Minty's head instead, fracturing her skull and leaving her unconscious. She never saw a doctor for her injuries, and she never fully recovered. For the rest of her life, Minty suffered from spells, where she would seem to fall asleep. Doctors now believe this was probably undiagnosed epilepsy caused by the head injury. She also had visions, which she interpreted as messages from God.

Despite the injury, Minty continued on with her life, and at age twenty-two, she married John Tubman. At that point she also began to go by her mother's first name, Harriet.

The life of an enslaved person was always unpredictable, but Harriet felt particularly vulnerable in 1849 when her master died. She was afraid of being sold and separated from her family. The only option she saw was to run away. Her husband refused to go with her, so she convinced two of her brothers, Henry and Ben, to join her. On the night of September 17, 1849, they ran away, but Henry and Ben became overwhelmed by fear. They turned back and forced Harriet to go with them.

THE UNDERGROUND RAILROAD

The Underground Railroad was neither underground nor a railroad. It was a secret network of routes and safe houses used by enslaved African Americans to escape to free states, Canada, Mexico, and overseas. It operated from the late eighteenth century to the Civil War and helped as many as 100,000 people find freedom. It was called a railroad because it used the same terminology, such as "conductors" (guides), "stations" (hiding places), and "passengers" (runaways).

People typically traveled ten to twenty miles at night and hid during the day in barns, under church floors, and in caves or other secret locations. Each conductor typically knew only a small part of the network, so that no individual could put the entire system at risk.

But Harriet wasn't willing to give up on her freedom. Several days later, she ran again, this time without telling anyone about her plans. "There are two things I've got a right to, and these are, Death or Liberty—one or the other I mean to have," she said. "No one will take me back alive; I shall fight for my liberty, and when the time has come for me to go, the Lord will let them kill me."

Traveling at night, Harriet sneaked from one safe house to another, following the Underground Railroad. But she did not rest when she arrived in Pennsylvania as a free woman. Instead, she decided to return to Maryland to help others escape. On her first trip back, she helped her niece and her niece's children escape. She offered to assist her husband, but he had remarried and wanted to stay.

During a period of about ten years, Harriet guided at least seventy enslaved men, women, and children to freedom. She also helped about sixty more people escape to Canada. She earned the name Black Moses because she led her people to freedom, similar to Moses in the Bible. "I never lost a passenger," she said.

When the Civil War broke out in 1861, Harriet volunteered to help the Union army. At first, she worked as a cook, laundress, and nurse, but the Union officers soon realized that Harriet would make an excellent spy. She was familiar with the landscape and savvy about traveling, and she also had the trust and respect of other African Americans who were reluctant to work with armed white soldiers, even those from the North.

Over time, Harriet set up a vast spy network of former slaves. African Americans were excellent intelligence collectors because they were largely underestimated and ignored by whites. Harriet knew how important former slaves could be in the war effort, but she also

appreciated the risk she was asking her people to assume: anyone caught spying for the Union army would be hanged.

In addition to collecting information, Harriet worked side by side with Colonel James Montgomery to plan a raid on the plantations along the Combahee River in South Carolina. On June 2, 1863, three Union ships and about 150 black soldiers

This painting by artist Charles T. Webber (1825-1911) shows enslaved people escaping on the Underground Railroad with the support of white farmers.

began their journey along the winding river. The Confederate forces had studded the river with explosives, but Harriet's spies knew the river because they had piloted boats along the water when transporting rice and cotton from the plantations to the ports. The African American soldiers were able to avoid the hidden explosives, or locate and disarm them.

When slaves working in the rice and cotton fields saw Union ships approach, they rushed toward the river. The Union forces welcomed the slaves aboard and then took as much rice, corn, cotton, and livestock as they could carry. What they could not take with them, the soldiers destroyed, burning the plantations and fields behind them. Not only did this leave the Confederates with less food and fewer supplies, it also struck an emotional blow by destroying some of the wealthiest plantations in the South. In this raid, Harriet became the first and only woman to lead a group of men in battle during the Civil War.

The attack was a remarkable success. During that single operation, Harriet helped free an astonishing 756 enslaved men, women, and children—ten times more people than she had been able to help during her work on the Underground Railroad.

Despite her contributions to the war effort, Harriet was not paid for her military service. She supported herself during the war by selling pies and root beer to the troops.

After the war, Harriet married a Civil War veteran and moved to Auburn, New York. She had trouble collecting a pension, but she was finally successful sometime in the 1880s. In her later years, Harriet founded the Harriet Tubman Home for the Aged. After undergoing brain surgery to treat the ongoing symptoms caused by her childhood injury, Harriet had to move into the home herself in 1911. She died of pneumonia on March 10, 1913, and was buried with military honors at Fort Hill Cemetery in Auburn.

Harriet Tubman in a photograph taken around 1885. The exact date of Tubman's birth is unknown. She reported her birth year as 1820, 1822, and 1825, evidence that she had only a basic idea of the year of her birth.

SARAH ROSETTA WAKEMAN:
SHE KEPT HER SECRET TO THE END

SARAH ROSETTA
WAKEMAN

Unlike most women who enlisted as men in order to join the military, Sarah Rosetta Wakeman took her assumed identity with her to the grave.

Sarah Wakeman—who went by her middle name, Rosetta—was born on January 16, 1843, in Bainbridge, New York. Her family was poor, and she was the oldest of nine children. So Rosetta left home early in her life to look for a job.

Rosetta quickly learned that she could make more money as a man than a woman, so she disguised herself as a man and took a job as a coal handler on a canal boat in Binghamton, New York. While working, she was approached by military recruiters who told her she could earn $13 a month, plus a $152 signing fee if she joined the army. On August 30, 1862,

The letters of Sarah Rosetta Wakeman offer a glimpse into the life of a female soldier during the Civil War. In one letter, she wrote, "I don't know how long before I shall have to go into the field of battle. For my part I don't care. I don't feel afraid to go."

she enlisted in Company H of the 153rd New York Infantry Regiment using the name Lyons Wakeman. Her enlistment records indicate that she was five feet tall with brown hair, blue eyes, and a light complexion.

Rosetta's regiment left for Washington, DC, about six weeks later. She worked on guard duty in Alexandria, Virginia, and on Capitol Hill. Her unit later went to Louisiana, where the soldiers marched hundreds of miles through the swamp. She and her regiment fought in several battles as part of the Red River Campaign.

Military life suited Rosetta. "I don't care anything about coming home," she wrote to her family after about a year in service. "I have enjoyed my self the best since I have been gone away from home than I ever did before in my life."

After the war she planned to buy a small farm of her own in Wisconsin, but she never got the chance. While still in the military, Rosetta and a number of other soldiers drank from a waterway that had been contaminated by dead animals further upstream. She and many other soldiers became sick. On May 3, 1864, Rosetta was hospitalized for chronic diarrhea. She was transferred to a hospital in New Orleans but nothing could be done to save her. She died on June 19, 1864.

Rosetta was buried at Chalmette National Cemetery near New Orleans in a grave marked Private Lyons Wakeman. While she was in the hospital, no one had discovered that she was a woman, or if the nurses had learned the truth in her final days, no one revealed her secret. Most likely, the soldiers were overwhelmed by the number of dead to bury, so they probably paid little attention to her after she died.

Rosetta had written a number of letters home during her service in the army. The family had bundled the letters and placed them in the attic of the family home, where they were forgotten for more than one hundred years. In 1976, a relative discovered the letters, and in 1994 they were published in a book titled, *An Uncommon Soldier: The Civil War Letters of Sarah Rosetta Wakeman, alias, Pvt. Lyons Wakeman, 153rd Regiment, New York State Volunteers, 1862–1864.*

DR. MARY EDWARDS WALKER:
MEDAL OF HONOR WINNER

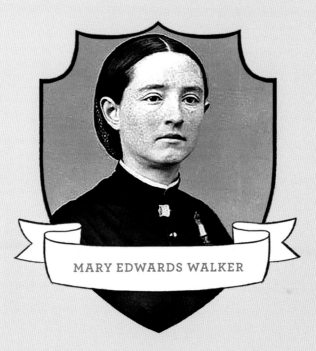

MARY EDWARDS WALKER

D r. Mary Edwards Walker did things her own way. She was an independent thinker, unafraid of taking a stand. The youngest of seven children, Mary was born in Oswego, New York, on November 26, 1832. Her parents were progressives who believed that girls deserved a good education, the freedom to think for themselves, and the confidence to question authority.

She lived up to her parents' expectations. As a child she read her father's books on anatomy and physiology, which sparked a lifelong interest in medicine. When she was twenty-one years old, she enrolled at Syracuse Medical College, now the State University of New York Upstate Medical University, where she graduated with honors in 1855. She was the only woman in her class.

Of nearly 3,500 Congressional Medal of Honor recipients, Dr. Mary Edwards Walker is the only woman and one of only eight civilians to receive the honor.

While in medical school, Walker met and married fellow student Albert Miller. She broke with the customs of the time and refused to include the word "obey" in her wedding vows; she also continued to use her maiden name, instead of taking her husband's name. The newlyweds set up a medical practice in Rome, New York, but many people weren't willing to accept advice from a female doctor. Her husband was not faithful to her, and they divorced in 1869 after a fourteen-year marriage.

Throughout her life, Walker dressed in untraditional clothes. She considered long skirts unhygienic because they dragged through dirt and mud. As a young girl on the farm and later as a doctor in medical practice, she wore knee-length dresses with pants underneath. Unlike other women who experimented with blousy loose pants, Walker wore straight-legged pants with suspenders, which she found less restricting. When accused of dressing like a man, she replied, "I don't wear men's clothes. I wear my own clothes."

At the beginning of the Civil War, she volunteered for the Union army. The military refused to accept female surgeons, so she took a civilian position as a nurse. She wanted to work where she was most needed, and she ended up near the front lines, serving at the First Battle of Bull Run in 1861 and later at the Patent Office Hospital in Washington, DC. Her skills were soon recognized, and her superiors eventually permitted her to work as a surgeon because they needed additional help.

In September 1863 she was hired as a contract assistant surgeon, becoming the first female surgeon of the United States Army. She was hired as a civilian doctor, meaning she didn't get military rank, and she was paid significantly less than the military doctors. She was later appointed acting assistant surgeon of the Fifty-Second Ohio Infantry.

As a doctor, Walker often crossed battle lines to provide medical care. When she went behind enemy lines to perform surgery, she didn't carry any weapons to show that she came in peace. But the enemy didn't always trust her. On April 10, 1864, as soon as Walker finished helping a Confederate doctor perform an amputation, she was arrested as a Union spy because she was found on enemy territory. She was taken to Dalton, Georgia, and then forced to walk seven hundred miles to Castle Thunder, a prison in Richmond, Virginia. Along the way, people came out to stare at the "lady physician in bloomers." She also wore a green sash around her waist, indicating that she was a surgeon. After four months in prison, she was released in a prisoner exchange between the North and South, and she continued with her medical service.

After the war, President Andrew Johnson awarded Walker the Congressional Medal of Honor for valor in battle in 1865. The Congressional Medal of Honor is the highest American decoration awarded to military service members who distinguish themselves with acts of valor on the battlefield. For more than fifty years, Walker proudly wore her medal, but in 1917, Congress changed the rules for the award and stripped Walker and 910 other Medal of Honor recipients of the honor, claiming that she did not earn the medal because she did not serve in battle. Walker refused to return the medal, arguing that she had earned the recognition by going into enemy territory to serve patients when the male doctors refused to do so. In 1977 President Jimmy Carter reinstated Walker's name on the official list of Medal of Honor recipients.

Walker did receive a disability pension for eye problems she suffered as a result of her time as a prisoner of war. She was awarded $8.50 a month starting in 1865, and in 1899 the amount was raised to $20.

As a veteran, Walker became a writer and lecturer, speaking about issues of concern to her, including health care, temperance, women's rights, suffrage, and dress reform.

Walker died on February 21, 1919, at the age of eighty-six. She was buried at Rural Cemetery in Oswego, New York, wearing a black pantsuit with an American flag draped over her casket.

CATHAY WILLIAMS:
FROM SLAVE TO SOLDIER

CATHAY WILLIAMS

Cathay Williams—who joined the military as William Cathay—was the first known African American woman to dress as a man and enlist in the army.

Cathay Williams was born in Independence, Missouri, in September 1844. Her father was free but her mother was a slave, so she was considered the property of her mother's owner. Williams grew up in slavery and worked as a house slave on a plantation near Jefferson City, Missouri.

In 1861, when Williams was seventeen years old, the Union forces occupied Jefferson City. Rather than freeing the enslaved people, Williams and other former slaves were forced to serve as cooks, nurses, and laundry workers for the military, but they were paid wages

The image comes from a painting of Cathay Williams by William Jennings for the U.S. Army.

for their work. For several years, Williams served with the Eighth Indiana Volunteer Infantry Regiment, following the forces through Georgia, Louisiana, and Virginia.

When the Civil War ended, there were few jobs open to African American women, especially in the South. When a female cousin and a good female friend told Cathay they were going to dress as men and enlist in the military, she decided to join, too. There weren't many other employment options that offered stable pay, health care, and a pension.

Williams's enlistment papers described her as five feet, nine inches tall, with black hair, black eyes, and a black complexion. She was twenty-two years old on November 15, 1866, when she enlisted for a three-year engagement with Company A of the Thirty-Eighth Infantry, one of four all-black regiments formed that year. (She is the only woman known to have dressed as a man and enlisted in her unit.) Her unit was ordered to the West, where Williams and the other soldiers fought against the Native Americans. The Plains Indians named the African American soldiers "Buffalo Soldiers" because they had short curly hair like buffaloes and they were strong and courageous fighters. The nickname was intended to express honor and respect.

Not long after beginning her service, Williams contracted smallpox. She suffered repeated bouts of serious illness and was often hospitalized. Within two years, the regimental doctor learned that she was a woman, and she was discharged on October 14, 1868.

After her discharge, Cathay worked various jobs, including as a cook at Fort Union, New Mexico, and as a seamstress and a boarding house manager in Colorado. Years later a newspaper reporter learned about her military service as a man and wrote an article about her life that was published in the *St. Louis Daily Times* on January 2, 1876.

Williams never recovered her health. In 1891 she applied for a military disability pension, but her request was denied. While the date of Williams's death is unknown, historians believe she died sometime in 1893, not long after the government rejected her request for assistance. It is believed that her grave was marked with a wooden sign that decomposed long ago, so her final resting place remains a mystery still today.

A NEW KIND OF SOLDIER:

WOMEN IN THE SPANISH-AMERICAN WAR AND WORLD WAR I

After the Civil War, the country needed time to heal. The fighting between the North and South devastated families and communities, and it took many years to recover and rebuild. The next major military engagement, the Spanish-American War, was not fought until the close of the nineteenth century, in 1898.

During the Spanish-American War, the military finally began to recognize that women could play an important part in a professionalized nursing corps. Congress authorized the army to hire female nurses and pay them $30 a month, but these women were not given military status or benefits. From 1898 to 1901, almost 1,600 women served as military nurses in the United States, at U.S. bases around the world, and on hospital ships.

But despite the efforts to improve sanitation and establish good medical practices, the working conditions were poor for nurses. Typhoid fever spread quickly through the camps and infected both soldiers and health care providers. Ellen May Tower of Byron, Michigan, holds the unfortunate distinction of being the first army nurse to die on foreign soil; she died of typhoid fever while serving in Puerto Rico during the

THE SPANISH-AMERICAN WAR (APRIL 21, 1898– AUGUST 13, 1898)

The Spanish-American War was fought in Cuba, Puerto Rico, Guam, and the Philippines between the United States and Spain. The battle began when America intervened in the Cuban War of Independence. The war resulted not only in Cuban independence from Spain but also in Puerto Rico, Guam, and the Philippine Islands becoming American territories. The United States entered the fighting after the USS *Maine* was sunk in Havana Harbor, Cuba.

Spanish-American War and before Puerto Rico became a U.S. territory. Her body was returned to the United States, where she also became the first woman to receive a military funeral when she was buried in her hometown in Michigan.

After the Spanish-American War, the official role of women in the military began to drastically change for the better. And while it was a slow change, improvements were being made. Leaders in the armed forces started to see the value of a trained

WORLD WAR I (1917–1918)

World War I—also called the First World War, the Great War, or the War to End All Wars—was the first global war. The fighting followed the assassination of Archduke Franz Ferdinand of Austria, which set off a diplomatic crisis across Europe. It lasted from July 28, 1914, to November 11, 1918; the United States entered the war in 1917. More than seventy million soldiers took part and more than nine million soldiers and seven million civilians died worldwide in what proved to be one of the deadliest conflicts in history. The high death count is due, in part, to the fact that weapons of war had become more technologically sophisticated, with the creation of barbed wire, machine guns, tanks, and poison gas. World War I was politically significant because it resulted in the demise of the German Empire, the Russian Empire, the Austro-Hungarian Empire, and the Ottoman Empire; national boundaries were redrawn in Europe as part of the peace process.

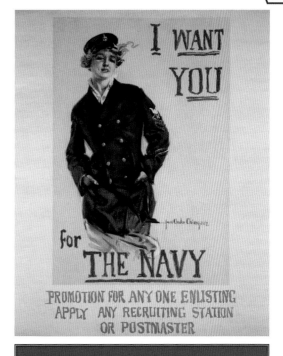

A U.S. recruiting poster for women to enlist in the navy during war

professional nursing staff, and they moved to make female nurses a permanent part of the military.

In 1901, the United States established the Army Nurse Corps, and in 1908 it established the Navy Nurse Corps. The women who served as military nurses wore uniforms and were attached to military units, but they were still considered civilians. They didn't have rank, and they didn't receive retirement pensions or disability benefits, even if they were injured in the line of duty.

During World War I, more than 21,000 women served in the Army Nurse Corps, and 1,500 more served in the Navy Nurse Corps. And for the first time, women worked in non-nursing jobs, too. The navy began to need additional help with its clerical and administrative work. So in 1916, Secretary of the Navy Josephus Daniels famously asked, "Is there any law that says a yeoman must be a man?" A yeoman is an enlisted soldier in the navy who does administrative or clerical work.

After checking the regulations, an officer told Daniels that there was no such rule.

And in that moment, Daniels made a decision that would change the role of women in the military: he decided to allow women to join the Naval Reserve.

In 1917, the first women joined the navy. Most did clerical jobs, but some worked as radio operators, electricians, pharmacists, photographers, telegraphers, fingerprint experts, chemists, torpedo assemblers, and camouflage designers, and other skilled noncombat positions. These female soldiers received the *same* pay—$28.75 per month— and the *same* veterans' benefits as men. This proved to be a huge step forward in welcoming women into the military.

And the idea caught on! During World

Women working with explosives at an ammunition factory in Nottinghamshire, UK, in July 1917

★★★ CANARIES IN A FACTORY

The women who worked in munitions factories often handled TNT—trinitrotoluene—an explosive chemical that caused their skin to turn an orange-yellow color. These workers, sometimes called "canary girls" because of their skin discoloration, often worked with these poisonous chemicals without protective clothing or masks. Many experienced nausea, skin irritation, and liver damage. The problem was particularly bad in England, where at least one hundred women died during World War I from exposure to TNT in factory work.

War I, the navy employed 11,274 female yeomen. In 1918, the marines also began enlisting women in noncombat roles. Ultimately 305 women joined and served in the Marine Corps Reserve during World War I.

On the home front, women who did not serve in the military also found new economic opportunities. Many took jobs left open when men went to fight in the war. The rate of employment among American women increased from 24 percent in 1914 to more than 40 percent in 1918. Many of these women worked in what had been considered male jobs, such as postal workers, police, firefighters, bus and tram conductors, and bank tellers. In many cases, women did the same work for half the wages paid to men.

New jobs were also created to support the war effort, such as line jobs in munitions factories. In fact, the demand for weapons made munitions factories the largest single employer of women in 1918. With so many men pulled out of the workforce to serve in the military, there was no choice but to allow women to work in nontraditional jobs.

★★★ WHAT ARE THE RESERVES?

The reserves are military units made up of trained soldiers who continue with their civilian lives and careers, but they are on call to serve if needed. Reservists receive the same basic training as full-time soldiers, but they return to their homes and their private lives rather than going into active duty. They spend one weekend a month, plus two weeks a year, training with their unit. They typically serve for three to six years.

EDITH AYRES AND HELEN WOOD:
THE FIRST TO DIE

Edith Ayres and Helen Wood were the first enlisted women to die in the line of military duty.

Once women had the right to serve in the military, they ran the risk of dying in service. On May 20, 1917, two army nurses—Edith Ayres and Helen Wood—became the first female members of the military to sacrifice their lives in the line of duty during World War I.

Edith Work Ayres was born in 1880 in Attica, Ohio. After her husband died in 1906, she went to Chicago to become a nurse. She graduated from the Illinois Training School for nurses in 1913 and took a job at the Cook County Hospital in Illinois as a head nurse. In 1917, she volunteered with the Red Cross and was assigned to go to France.

Helen Burnet Wood was born in Portobello, Scotland, in 1888. She was the oldest of seven children—she had three sisters and three brothers. Two of her brothers were killed serving Scotland in the war. She came to the United States and studied nursing in Evanston, Illinois, at the Evanston Hospital Training School. She then volunteered with U.S. Army Base Hospital No. 12, also known as the Northwestern University Base Hospital.

Helen and Edith died on board the SS *Mongolia* on their way to France. During a practice drill, one of the guns on the ship exploded and shell fragments immediately killed Ayres and Wood, who were standing on the deck. They became the first nurses to die during service in World War I.

GENEVIEVE AND LUCILLE BAKER:
ALWAYS READY

Since the 1830s women had been serving in the coast guard as civilian lighthouse keepers, but women weren't allowed to formally enlist and wear the military uniform until 1918. The first two women to join the coast guard were nineteen-year-old twin sisters Genevieve and Lucille Baker.

The Bakers were born in Brooklyn, New York, on February 28, 1900. Their parents were Polish immigrants who changed the family name from Waclawski to Baker. Lucille and Genevieve worked in clerical positions at the Brooklyn Navy Yard before they enlisted. They had two brothers who were serving as soldiers in France.

According to policy, female coast guard recruits had to be between eighteen and thirty-five years old, healthy, of good character, and of neat appearance. There were no education requirements, but recruiters preferred high school graduates or women with business or office experience.

Twins Lucille and Genevieve Baker in 1918

The Baker twins had experience as bookkeepers, skills that were needed when they enlisted in the Naval Defense Reserve and became the first yeomanettes. At the time, the military needed women to perform administrative tasks so that the men who had been doing those jobs could transfer to combat positions. During World War I, the twins worked as bookkeepers and telephone operators.

Both sisters received an honorable discharge and veterans' benefits following their service. Lucille Baker Steffen died in 1968; Genevieve Baker French died in 1999.

ESTHER VOORHEES HASSON:
ARMY, NAVY, ARMY

ESTHER
VOORHEES HASSON

During her career, Esther Voorhees Hasson served in the Army Nurse Corps *and* the Navy Nurse Corps.

Esther was born in Baltimore, Maryland, on September 20, 1867. After graduating from the Connecticut Training School for Nurses in New Haven in 1897, she became a nurse with the army and served on the hospital ship USS *Relief* during the Spanish-American War. During that mission, she was one of six nurses who were responsible for tending almost 1,500 sick and wounded soldiers.

After the war, Hasson served as a military nurse in the Philippines for several years before leaving the army in 1901. She returned to the United States but rejoined the military as a

Esther Voorhees Hasson was the first superintendent of the Navy Nurse Corps. She also served in the Army Nurse Corps during the Spanish-American War and World War I.

nurse in Panama from 1905 to 1907.

When Hasson learned that the navy was going to form a nurse corps, she applied to become superintendent of the new division. Few people applied for the job. Hasson was chosen, and she returned to the United States in 1908 to become the first superintendent of the Navy Nurse Corps. In her new role, Hasson established the rules and expectations for the nursing program and recruited and trained eighty-five female nurses.

Hasson had lofty ambitions for the Navy Nurse Corps. In an article published in the *American Journal of Nursing* in 1909, Hasson wrote:

"It is too soon as yet to outline the scope of the work or to make predictions as to the future of the corps, but it is my most earnest hope to make it a dignified, respected body of women.... We nurses who come into the nursing service of the Navy during this first year of its existence are the pioneers, and it rests with us to make the traditions and to set the pace for those who are to follow."

Hasson left the Navy Nurse Corps in 1911. But when the United States entered the war in 1917, she returned to the military once again, this time as an Army Reserve nurse. Hasson died on March 8, 1942, at age seventy-four in Washington, DC.

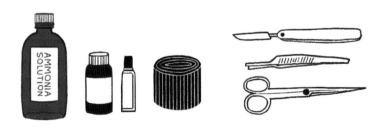

LENAH HIGBEE:
THE NAVY'S NURSE

LENAH HIGBEE

Two years after the end of World War I, the navy awarded the Navy Cross—the second-highest navy award for valor in combat—to four heroic women, all nurses with the Navy Nurse Corps. Only one woman, Lenah Higbee, attended the award ceremony on November 11, 1920, and became the first living female to receive the honor. The other three nurses—Louise Hidell, Edna Place, and Lillian Murphy—had died after contracting the Spanish flu while caring for their patients.

Lenah Sutcliffe was born on May 18, 1874, in Chatham, New Brunswick, Canada. She moved to the United States in 1899 to go to nursing school at the New York Postgraduate Hospital. She married Marine Corps lieutenant colonel John Henley Higbee and became a U.S. citizen. Her husband died in 1908, the same year that President Theodore Roosevelt signed a bill authorizing the creation of the Navy Nurse Corps. Higbee wanted to do something to give new meaning to her life, so she traveled to Washington, DC, at her own expense to apply to become a navy nurse. She passed the written and oral exams and was chosen to be one of the first twenty nurses admitted to the nursing corps. These twenty nurses were the first women to serve as official members of the navy.

In 1911, after three years of serving, Higbee was promoted to superintendent of the Navy

First Twenty Navy Nurses Appointed in 1908.

The Sacred Twenty were the first twenty women to serve in the Navy Nurse Corps. Lenah Higbee is the sixth from the left in the front row.

THE SACRED TWENTY

The Sacred Twenty were the first female members of the Navy Nurse Corps. They were required to be unmarried American women between the ages of twenty-two and forty-four. The nurses—all white—came from a number of different nursing schools and had a range of skills.

After going to nursing school, members of the Navy Nurse Corps received additional training at the U.S. Naval Hospital in Washington, DC. They were assigned to hospitals in Washington, New York, Virginia, and Maryland, as well as U.S. naval hospitals in Guam, Samoa, and the Philippines. The nurses had to provide their own room and board during the term of their service.

Nurse Corps. She replaced Esther Voorhees Hasson, who'd retired in 1911. The corps grew under Lenah's direction and in response to the demands of war. Between 1917 and 1918 the number of nurses serving in the corps increased from 160 to 1,386.

In addition to treating soldiers injured in battle, Higbee and the other nurses in the corps had to treat people sickened by the Spanish flu, a pandemic that killed about fifty million people worldwide. In the navy and marines, thousands of soldiers came down with the Spanish flu and needed treatment.

Higbee resigned from the navy in 1922, after eleven years heading the corps. During her service, she focused on publicizing and enhancing the reputation of the Nurse Corps. She published articles in professional journals about the role of nursing in the military and good medical practices, and she encouraged other nurses to do so as well. She died at age sixty-six in Winter Park, Florida, on January 10, 1941.

OPHA MAY JOHNSON:
THE FIRST FEMALE MARINE

OPHA MAY JOHNSON

Not much is known about Opha May Johnson, but one central fact stands out: she was the first woman to enlist in the Marine Corps Women's Reserve during World War I.

Opha May Jacob was born in Kokomo, Indiana, in 1879. She was a speedy typist who graduated from the shorthand and typewriting department of Wood's Commercial College in 1895. A few years later, she married Victor H. Johnson, musical director of the Lafayette Square Opera House; they did not have children. Opha Johnson put her skills to work as a typist and clerk at a government agency.

In the early years of World War I, the Marine Corps remained an all-male force. But by

1918, the Marine Corps, much like the army and navy, needed help with administrative tasks so that the men who had been doing that work could serve in combat assignments overseas. In order to fill these positions, the military decided to allow women to enlist in the Marine Corps Reserve for the first time. This meant that women could serve in the military, even though they did not yet have the right to vote.

When the call went out for new recruits, several thousand women applied, and 305 were chosen. The first to volunteer was thirty-nine-year-old Opha Johnson. On August 13, 1918, she became the first official female marine.

Opha was posted as a clerk at the Marine Corps headquarters in Arlington, Virginia. In addition to performing clerical duties, she and the other female marines had to drill and train. The drill sergeants weren't thrilled with having female recruits, and some disparagingly referred to them as marinettes. The women didn't like the nickname. "Anybody that calls me anything but 'Marine' is going to hear from me," said another female marine who was serving at the time.

When the war ended, Johnson and the other female marines were released from their posts. Johnson became a clerk in the War Department. She also joined the American Legion, a veterans' organization, that had established a separate post for the female marine reservists. About 90 of the 305 female marines joined the group.

She died at Mount Alto Veterans Hospital in Washington, DC, on August 11, 1955—exactly thirty-seven years after she first enlisted as a marine.

DR. ANITA NEWCOMB MCGEE:
CREATING A PROFESSIONAL NURSING CORPS

ANITA NEWCOMB MCGEE

Anita Newcomb McGee was a medical doctor who helped improve and standardize nursing care for the military during the Spanish-American War.

Anita Newcomb was born on November 4, 1864, in Washington, DC. She graduated from high school in 1882 and spent three years traveling overseas and attending classes in history and genealogy in England and Switzerland. When she returned home, she married William J. McGee in 1888 and began studying medicine, although few women became doctors at that time. She was an excellent student, scoring at the top of her class in dermatology and second in clinical medicine. She graduated from medical school at Columbian College (now George Washington University) in 1892 and then completed a postgraduate course in gynecology at

Johns Hopkins University School of Medicine before starting in private medical practice.

Dr. McGee was active in the American Association for the Advancement of Science, the Women's Anthropological Society of America, and the Daughters of the American Revolution. When the Spanish-American War began in 1898, she learned that the army surgeon general planned to allow only fully qualified nurses to serve. Dr. McGee left her private medical practice to support the war effort by founding and directing the Daughters of the American Revolution Hospital Corps, a group that trained volunteer nurses for service in the army and navy.

In August 1898, she became an official part of the military when she was appointed acting assistant surgeon general in the army. Her job was to train and organize the 1,600 army nurses who served during the war. She was the only woman to directly serve in the military and the only female allowed to wear an officer's uniform.

The Spanish-American War lasted only three months, three weeks, and two days. After the war, Dr. McGee pushed to have the military establish a permanent corps that would be staffed by fully qualified nurses. To achieve that goal, she helped to write the Army Reorganization Act of 1901, which resulted in the formation of a permanent Army Nurse Corps. She was an excellent organizer and also wrote the manual on nursing for the military. In her free time, she led the effort to fund and build the Spanish-American War Nurses Memorial at Arlington National Cemetery.

Dr. McGee organized the Society of Spanish-American War Nurses in 1900 and served as the organization's president for six years. She received the Spanish War Service Medal from the U.S. Army for her service. When the Russo-Japanese War began in 1904, she and a group of nine nurses offered to go to Japan to help the Japanese government form its own professional nursing corps. For this, she was awarded the Japanese Imperial Order of the Precious Crown by the Japanese government and the Silver Special Members' Badge by the Japanese Red Cross.

After returning to the United States, Dr. McGee lectured about nursing and hygiene at the University of California, Berkeley. Dr. McGee died on October 5, 1940. She was buried next to her father in Arlington National Cemetery with full military honors.

LORETTA PERFECTUS WALSH:
A NEW KIND OF SOLDIER

LORETTA PERFECTUS
WALSH

L oretta Perfectus Walsh helped to redefine the role of women in the military. When she enlisted in the Naval Reserve on March 17, 1917, she became the first woman to serve in the armed forces as anything other than a nurse.

Loretta Walsh was born in Philadelphia, Pennsylvania, in 1896. As a young woman, she carefully followed the global events that contributed to the beginning of World War I. International tensions grew in March 1917 when a German U-boat attacked American ships, killing fifteen Americans. The situation became more heated when the military ordered that American merchant ships be armed and ready to fight if they encountered the U-boats. As these events were unfolding, Walsh learned that the navy was going to

change its policies and allow women to enlist.

And on March 17, 1917, they did! The Navy Department opened its ranks to women, and twenty-year-old Walsh was the first to heed the call. She signed on for a four-year enlistment as a yeoman.

The titles for female recruits got a bit fuzzy. Walsh enlisted as a yeoman (F)—F for female—but female yeomen were sometimes called yeomanettes or yeowomen. Female yeomen performed clerical work, serving as typists, stenographers, bookkeepers, accountants, telephone operators, and inventory control experts. Other females in the navy became radio operators, electricians, draftsmen, fingerprint experts, and other technical specialists. Several weeks after Walsh was sworn in, Congress declared war—the United States joined World War I. More than 11,000 women served in these and other roles in the navy.

While the war with the Germans ended on November 11, 1918, Walsh and other female yeomen continued to work for several months longer. But by the end of July 1919, a month after the Treaty of Versailles officially ended World War I, the female yeomen were decommissioned because they were no longer needed. Walsh remained on inactive reserve status until the end of her four-year enlistment.

Walsh suffered from a serious case of the Spanish flu during the pandemic of 1918. A few years later she developed tuberculosis. She died on August 6, 1925, at the age of twenty-nine.

IT'S OUR WAR, TOO:

WOMEN IN WORLD WAR II

After World War I ended, women turned their attention to a different battle: the fight to be recognized as full citizens by gaining the right to vote. After more than seventy years of campaigning for suffrage, women *finally* got the right to vote in 1920.

Women's work during the war—both in the military and at home—made it difficult for legislators to dismiss women's call for suffrage. After a great deal of public pressure from women in the suffrage movement, President Woodrow Wilson finally decided to support women's right to vote. In an address to the Senate in 1918, President Wilson said, "We have made partners of the women in this war; shall we admit them only to a partnership of suffering and sacrifice and toil and not to a partnership of privilege, and right?" Later that year, Congress passed the Nineteenth Amendment to the Constitution giving women the right to vote, and in 1920 it became law after two-thirds of the states ratified the amendment.

The changes with women's role in society didn't stop with suffrage. In the period known as the Roaring Twenties, many women rejected traditional female roles and embraced the modern era. During this

WORLD WAR II
(1939–1945)

World War II was fought between the Allies (including the United States, United Kingdom, Soviet Union, China, France, Poland, Australia, and Canada, among others) and the Axis nations (Germany, Japan, Italy, among others). It involved more than thirty countries and left fifty to eighty-five million people dead. It began when Nazi Germany invaded Poland in 1939. At the same time, Japan tried to dominate Asia in the Pacific, opening up the Pacific Theater, another area of fighting. When the war ended, the United States and the Soviet Union emerged as the two world superpowers.

time, more Americans moved to the cities and the nation grew wealthier. People bought cars, telephones, and electric appliances as part of the emerging consumer culture. This period of prosperity abruptly ended with the stock market crash of 1929, which triggered the Great Depression and defined the 1930s.

After struggling through a decade of economic despair, the economy began to recover and the nation went to war. And, once again, women were a critical part of the military mission. During World War II, it became clear that women could—and should—play a significant role in the armed forces. Military leaders didn't experience a sudden change of heart about women. Instead, they experienced a basic manpower shortage. Every man was needed on the front lines, so women were brought into the military to fill the noncombat positions that had once been assigned to men. "Free a man to fight" became a rallying call for women in all branches of the armed forces.

While women were not considered for combat roles, they did take on a number of jobs that would have once been considered inappropriate. In addition to clerical and administrative work, they were now allowed to work in more technical roles, such as mechanics, pilots, and electricians, as well as skilled work, such as postal workers, parachute riggers, and many other jobs that did not directly involve fighting. One by one, all the branches of the armed forces opened their doors to women. Each had a different name for its recruits:

The insignia of the Women's Army Corps

In 1942, the army established the Women's Army Auxiliary Corps (WAAC), which changed its name to the Women's Army Corps (WAC) in 1943. More than 140,000 women enlisted and served as WACs during World War II.

The insignia of the WAVES

In 1942, the navy set up a women's auxiliary known as Women Accepted for Volunteer Emergency Service (WAVES). Nearly 90,000 women enlisted as WAVES.

The Marine Corps Women's Reserve insignia

In 1942, the Marine Corps founded the Marine Corps Women's Reserve (WR). More than 20,000 women served in more than 225 different specialties during World War II.

Air Force WASP badge

In 1942, pilots served in the army because the air force had not yet been established. That same year, the army formed the Women's Auxiliary Ferrying Squadron (WAFS), a group of female civilian transport pilots. In 1943, the WAFS were renamed the Women

Airforce Service Pilots (WASP). More than 1,000 female pilots served as WASPs. During the war, they flew more than 60 million miles in every type of military aircraft. Thirty-eight women died flying in noncombat missions.

Coast Guard emblem

In 1942, the coast guard established the Coast Guard Women's Reserve of the U.S. Coast Guard Reserve program. These women were called SPARs, which was derived from the first letters of the coast guard motto, *Semper paratus* (Always ready). More than 12,000 enlisted women served as SPARs during World War II.

BEA ARTHUR

Actress Bea Arthur—star of the sitcoms *Maude* (1970–1978) and *The Golden Girls* (1985–1992)—spent thirty months in the Marine Corps Women's Reserve working as a typist and truck driver. She enlisted in 1943 at age twenty-one; at the time her name was Bernice Frankel. She was promoted to staff sergeant and honorably discharged in September 1945 at the end of World War II.

Women's service during the war proved that they had a lot to offer the armed forces. The thousands of women who volunteered were essential in keeping the military running smoothly. Even though women did not engage in combat, sixteen female soldiers were killed by enemy fire during the war.

Women who did not join the military also supported the war effort by joining the civilian workforce, just as they did during World War I. Between 1940 and 1945, the number of women in the workforce increased from 27 percent to 37 percent. Many of these women worked in the aircraft industry and as munitions workers. Rosie the Riveter, the strong, red-bandanna-wearing factory worker, became a national icon of women in the workforce. Both men and women did their part: this was America's war.

Recruitment posters encouraged women to join the military during World War II.
The iconic *We Can Do It!* poster (top left) was designed by artist J. Howard Miller
(1918–2004) in 1942 for the War Production Coordinating Committee.

ANGELS OF BATAAN:
SERVING TO THE END

They were called the Angels of Bataan and the Battling Belles of Bataan, but another phrase could also describe them: prisoners of war.

During the early part of World War II, the Army Nurse Corps and Navy Nurse Corps stationed female nurses at hospitals in the Philippines. The Pacific War—also known as the War Against Japan—was the part of the war fought in the Pacific and Asia.

In 1941, the nurses in Bataan, a province near Manila, spent four months tending more than 6,000 sick and wounded U.S. soldiers in outdoor hospitals consisting of row after row of cots. Tropical diseases, like malaria and dysentery, were common among both the patients and nurses. The women did their best to care for their patients, despite the bombs falling around them.

In February 1945, the army and navy nurses from Bataan and Corregidor were freed after three years' imprisonment in Santo Tomas Internment Camp.

In April 1942, the fighting between the United States (and Allied nations) and Japan (and the Axis nations) escalated, and most of the nurses left Bataan and retreated to Corregidor, a nearby island, where they hid in a network of underground tunnels that had been built by the United States as a bombproof storage bunker. The nurses converted the facility into a 1,000-bed hospital with eight wards inside the mountain. On May 6, the entire island fell to Japanese control, and the nurses—sixty-six army nurses and eleven navy nurses—were taken as prisoners of war. They became the largest group of American women ever captured and imprisoned by any army.

The nurses were taken to Santo Tomas Internment Camp in Manila. Army major Maude C. Davison maintained command of the nurses, continuing with a routine of working four-hour shifts and wearing regular uniforms. While held at the camp, the nurses tended the 3,700 sick and injured soldiers who were also being held as prisoners of war.

Major Maude Davison served as chief nurse of the Army Nurse Corps during World War II.

In January 1944, the Japanese army took control of the internment camp from the Japanese civil forces. Once it became a military operation instead of a civilian one, food became very scarce and the women were forced to survive on near-starvation rations. During the next year of captivity, the prisoners lost an average of 30 percent of their body weight. Despite the harsh conditions and inadequate food, the nurses continued to tend to their patients and serve as a nursing unit.

American forces liberated the prisoners in February 1945. Although they were malnourished and many were sick, all seventy-seven nurses survived.

When they returned to the United States, the nurses were awarded Bronze Star Medals for valor and a Presidential Unit Citation for extraordinary heroic action.

MARGARET BOURKE-WHITE:
IMAGES OF WAR

MARGARET
BOURKE-WHITE

During her career Margaret Bourke-White took photographs all over the world, but among her most important images are the ones she took as the first official female photographer for the United States Army in World War II.

Margaret White was born in the Bronx, New York, on June 14, 1904. Her family moved to Bound Brook, New Jersey, where Margaret grew up as the middle child in a progressive household that encouraged determination and creativity. Her father was a photographer, and he often took Margaret with him on his assignments. She followed him around as he worked and pretended to take photographs with an empty cigar box, but her father did not teach Margaret how to use a camera. In fact, she did not use a camera until her mother gave

Margaret Bourke-White was the first female photographer for the army. Her coworkers at *Life* gave her the nickname Maggie the Indestructible because of her bravery and willingness to go into dangerous situations.

her one when she was an adult, after her father died.

Margaret attended seven universities and changed her field of study from herpetology—the study of reptiles and amphibians—to photography; she graduated from Cornell University in 1927. As a young woman she decided to change her name by hyphenating her mother's maiden name with her father's last name; she became Margaret Bourke-White. After graduation, she moved to Cleveland, Ohio, and opened a photography studio, specializing in architectural photography. Two years later, she took a job at *Fortune* magazine and improved her skills before becoming the first female photographer at *Life* magazine in 1936.

In 1941, she was the only foreign photographer present in Moscow when Germany invaded the Soviet Union. She captured the fighting on film. During World War II, *Life* magazine allowed Bourke-White to photograph the air force in action. Bourke-White became the first woman allowed to work in combat zones. She traveled with the Army Air Forces in North Africa, Italy, and Germany. In 1945, she went with General George S. Patton to the concentration camp at Buchenwald, capturing images that showed the world the horrors of the Holocaust.

"Using the camera was almost a relief," Bourke-White said. "It interposed a slight barrier between myself and the horror in front of me." The atrocities she witnessed may have also had personal significance: her family was Jewish and her father had grown up in Poland.

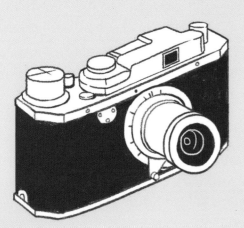

After the war, Bourke-White continued to photograph important events around the world, including the movement for Indian independence and the Korean War.

In 1952, Bourke-White developed symptoms of Parkinson's disease, a progressive neurological condition. She died August 27, 1971, at age sixty-seven. Her photographs are still important today and are displayed in the Brooklyn Museum, the Cleveland Museum of Art, the New Mexico Museum of Art, and the Museum of Modern Art.

JACQUELINE COCHRAN:
A RECORD-SHATTERING CAREER

JACQUELINE COCHRAN

Jacqueline Cochran—the "Speed Queen"—held more speed, distance, and altitude records than any other pilot of her day, male or female. Never satisfied, she would set a flying record one day, only to go back and break her own records again and again. She also used her skills in the skies to support her country by organizing the Women Airforce Service Pilots (WASPs) during World War II.

On May 11, 1906, Jacqueline was born in Pensacola, Florida, as Bessie Lee Pittman, but she began using the name Jackie when she was a teenager. At age fourteen, she married Robert Cochran, but the marriage didn't last.

In 1932, Cochran was invited by a friend to go to Miami. While on the trip, she met businessman Floyd Odlum. The two hit it off and were married a few years later.

Around the same time Cochran met Odlum, she also took her first ride in an airplane. She loved flying so much that she began taking flying lessons at Roosevelt Airfield on Long Island, New York, and earned her pilot's license in just three weeks. Within two years she had a commercial pilot's license. She loved speed, pushing herself and her aircraft to the limit. In 1935, she became the first woman to enter the Bendix Trophy Race, a transcontinental point-to-point airplane race. She came in third in 1937 and then went on to win the competition in 1938.

Colonel Jacqueline Cochran sits in the cockpit of a Curtiss P-40 Warhawk. In 1971, she became the first woman inducted into the National Aviation Hall of Fame in Dayton, Ohio.

Before the United States joined World War II, Cochran worked with Wings for Britain, an organization that flew American-built aircraft to England. She became the first woman to fly a bomber across the Atlantic. She volunteered with the British Royal Air Force and spent several months working with the British Air Transport Auxiliary, a group of female pilots who flew noncombat missions, freeing male pilots to join the fight.

Cochran wrote to first lady Eleanor Roosevelt suggesting the U.S. use female pilots in the Army Air Forces to cover routine assignments, like flying ambulance planes and transport flights, allowing men to fly combat missions. "In the field of aviation, the real 'bottle neck' in the long run is likely to be trained pilots," Cochran wrote.

When Cochran returned from England in 1943, she found that the military had already started a program similar to the one she suggested. A pilot had been hired to train the female pilots for the new program called the Women's Auxiliary Ferrying Squadron (WAFS), but Cochran wanted that job.

She lobbied the military to expand the program—and to hire her as the director. And in July 1943, the military agreed! Cochran became director of the Women Airforce Service Pilots (WASPs). During the war, more than 1,000 female pilots served as WASPs.

In recognition for her work in World War II, in 1945 Cochran became the first woman civilian to be awarded the Distinguished Service Medal, which was the highest noncombat award presented by the U.S. government at the time.

For several years after the war, Cochran worked as a correspondent for *Liberty* magazine, reporting on global events. But she missed flying so much that she returned to military life. In 1948, she was commissioned a lieutenant colonel in the Air Force Reserve, which allowed her to fly newer and faster aircraft. In 1953, Cochran became the first woman to fly faster than the speed of sound. She continued to set records in speed, altitude, and distance flying, breaking an astonishing seventy-three records in three years.

She was promoted to colonel in the Air Force Reserve in 1969, one year before she retired. Cochran died on August 9, 1980, age seventy-four, at her home in Indio, California.

CARMEN CONTRERAS-BOZAK:
THE FIRST HISPANIC WOMAN TO SERVE

CARMEN
CONTRERAS-BOZAK

World War II opened new opportunities not just for women but for minorities as well. In 1942, Carmen Contreras-Bozak became the first Hispanic woman to serve in the United States Women's Army Corps.

Carmen Contreras Torres was born on December 31, 1919, in Cayey, Puerto Rico. When she was a child, her parents divorced and Carmen moved to New York City with her mother and siblings. After completing high school and passing the civil service test—a written exam that was once required for federal employees—Carmen became a payroll clerk at the War Department in Washington, DC.

In 1942, the army was recruiting bilingual Hispanic women to help with the war effort because they needed help translating messages between English and Spanish. Carmen joined the Women's Army Auxiliary Corps. After training at Fort Lee, Virginia, she was sent to work as an interpreter and administrator with the 149th WAAC Post Headquarters Company in Algiers. One of her jobs was to translate encoded messages between headquarters and various other posts in the field. She was the first of nearly two hundred Puerto Rican women who would serve during the war.

After the war, Carmen was hospitalized for treatment of an eye infection she contracted while in Africa. While in the hospital she met Theodore John Bozak, a man who had been injured in combat. The two married and went on to have three children.

Contreras-Bozak lived in Florida and worked at the post office and as a real estate broker. Her military experience remained important to her throughout her life. She started a chapter of Women's Army Corps Veterans, as well as a chapter of the Society of Military Widows. She died on January 30, 2017, at age ninety-seven.

HISPANICS IN THE MILITARY

Hispanic Americans—those with ancestors from Spain, Mexico, the Caribbean, and Central and South America—have fought for the United States in every war since the Revolution. During the Civil War, thousands of Hispanic soldiers fought, representing both the Union and the Confederate sides.

In 1898, the United States acquired the territory of Puerto Rico at the end of the Spanish-American War. The following year, Congress authorized the formation of a new unit of soldiers, which later became the Sixty-Fifth Infantry Regiment. This group of mostly Hispanic soldiers from Puerto Rico fought in World War I, World War II, the Korean War, and in modern wars. In 2016, the Sixty-Fifth Infantry was awarded the Congressional Gold Medal for their service.

The statistics about Hispanics in the military are unreliable because Hispanic soldiers were categorized as white, rather than as a separate group, during most military history. Hispanics have served in both integrated and segregated military units. The last all-Puerto Rican unit was finally integrated in March 1953 during the Korean War.

Over the years, Hispanics have risen to the top military ranks. In 1964, Admiral Horacio Rivero, Jr., became the navy's first Hispanic four-star admiral. In 1982, General Richard E. Cavazos, a Mexican American, became the army's first Hispanic four-star general.

DR. MARGARET CRAIGHILL:
YES, WE CAN

MARGARET CRAIGHILL

As the first female commissioned officer in the United States Army Medical Corps, Dr. Margaret Craighill challenged the idea that women weren't suited for military service. Instead of seeing what women *couldn't* do, she recognized what they *could* do. During her service, Dr. Craighill advocated for expanded roles of women in the military, noting that women were already performing well in harsh climates and under difficult conditions.

Margaret Dorothea Craighill was born October 16, 1898, in Southport, North Carolina. She had an excellent academic résumé: she graduated Phi Beta Kappa—with high honors—from the University of Wisconsin in 1921 and earned her master's degree the following year.

Margaret Craighill traveled 56,000 miles over nine months to report on the conditions of army nurses and female service personnel. In recognition of her service during the war, Dr. Craighill was awarded the Legion of Merit.

She then attended the Johns Hopkins University School of Medicine, graduating in 1924. She spent the first part of her medical career in a variety of positions: teaching at Yale University, serving as an assistant resident of gynecology at Johns Hopkins Hospital, working as an assistant surgeon at Bellevue Hospital in New York City, running a private obstetrics and gynecology practice in Greenwich, Connecticut, and serving as dean of the Women's Medical College of Pennsylvania in Philadelphia.

As soon as President Franklin D. Roosevelt signed a bill allowing women to enter the Army and Navy Medical Corps, Dr. Craighill took notice. She came from a military family and she was eager to support the war effort. On May 28, 1943, Dr. Craighill became the first female commissioned officer in the Army Medical Corps. She served as the women's consultant to the surgeon general of the army, which made her responsible for commanding the Women's Health and Welfare Unit. As part of her job, she inspected the living conditions of women serving in the army, and she reviewed the screening process for women applying for service.

Typically, female enlistees were evaluated using the same health screenings as men. When Dr. Craighill took office, she developed a new procedure that included exams looking for pregnancy, tumors in reproductive organs, and other medical concerns facing women. Under her care, the rate of disability discharges dropped dramatically because women's health needs were finally being addressed at the time they enlisted.

Dr. Craighill also traveled to war zones in England, France, Italy, Egypt, Iran, China, and the Philippines, among other countries. She reported that women were performing their assigned jobs well, even under the extreme conditions. "Women have reached a situation where they should be judged by accomplishments and skill," she said.

On April 8, 1946, Dr. Craighill left the army. She returned to the Women's Medical College of Pennsylvania, and then she became a surgeon at Winter Veterans Hospital in Topeka, Kansas. She also consulted on issues involving medical care for female veterans. She did a lot for women's health at a time when the focus was still on men.

Later in her career she returned to private practice in Connecticut. She died June 20, 1977, at age seventy-eight in Southbury, Connecticut.

SUSAN AHN CUDDY:
THE FIRST ASIAN AMERICAN WOMAN IN THE NAVY

During World War II, Asian Americans faced significant discrimination. Nearly 120,000 Japanese American citizens were held in internment camps in the western United States, and nationwide almost all people of Asian descent were treated with prejudice and distrust. Even in such a suspicious and unwelcoming climate, Susan Ahn Cuddy overcame the prejudice and became the first Korean American woman to serve in the military and the first female navy gunnery officer.

SUSAN AHN CUDDY

In 1902, Susan's parents moved to the U.S. from Korea. Susan Ahn was born on January 16, 1915, in Los Angeles, California. Her parents were Korean independence activists who remained concerned about political issues in their homeland. The Ahn family helped other Korean immigrants settle in the United States, and their home became a gathering place for Korean activists who were working to free Korea from Japanese occupation.

Susan grew up hearing her parents criticize the Japanese, so when Japan bombed Pearl Harbor and drew the United States into World War II, she was eager to volunteer to do her part to support the war effort. In 1942, two years after graduating from San Diego State College, Susan enlisted in the Naval Reserve Midshipmen's School at Smith College, in Northampton, Massachusetts, becoming the first Asian American woman to join the navy.

In the navy, Susan became the first female aerial gunnery officer, teaching fighter pilots how to shoot down enemy aircraft. Most men respected her skills, but some stubborn soldiers didn't want to listen to advice from a woman—and they certainly didn't want to listen to an Asian American woman. But Susan put those soldiers in their place. Once when a white male pilot disobeyed her, she set him straight, telling him, "You will shoot when I tell you to shoot." She was his superior, and he listened.

In April 1947, Susan married Chief Petty Officer Francis X. Cuddy, an Irish American. Their marriage violated laws in place at the time that didn't allow people from different races to marry, but they were never prosecuted. Her husband was a code breaker who spoke Japanese fluently and his work helped in the effort to free Korea from Japanese control.

Susan Cuddy left the navy after the war and spent the rest of her career working for the National Security Agency in Washington, DC. She played an important role in many top secret projects to defend the United States against the Soviet Union during the Cold War. In 2006, she received the American Courage Award from the Asian American Justice Center in Washington, DC. Cuddy died at her home in Northridge, California, on June 24, 2015. She was one hundred years old.

The three Ahn siblings—Ralph, Philip, and Susan (*left to right*)—all served in the United States military during World War II.

CHARITY ADAMS EARLEY:
YOU'VE GOT MAIL

CHARITY
ADAMS EARLEY

Charity Adams Earley had one of the most important jobs in the military: she was responsible for mail delivery to seven million soldiers during World War II. For tired and lonely soldiers serving overseas, almost nothing could make them happier than a letter from home. Major Adams was also the first African American woman to be an officer in the Women's Army Auxiliary Corps, and she commanded the first battalion of African American women to serve overseas during World War II. By the end of the war, she was the highest-ranking African American woman in the army.

Charity Adams, the oldest of four children, was born on December 5, 1918, in Kitrell, North Carolina. She spent much of her childhood in Columbia, South Carolina, where her

"OVER MY DEAD BODY"

Charity Adams Earley had to endure segregation and overt racism when she was growing up in South Carolina in the 1920s and 1930s. By the time she enlisted in the army in 1942, she had grown considerably more outspoken.

In her 1989 memoir, *One Woman's Army: A Black Officer Remembers the WAC*, Major Adams recounted an experience with a general who criticized her when he was inspecting her battalion. When she told him that some of the women would not be present because they were working or sleeping after working the night shift, he responded, "I'm going to send a white first lieutenant down here to show you how to run this unit."

Adams replied, "Over my dead body, sir."

The general threatened to court-martial Adams. She threatened to file charges against him for disobeying an order from Allied headquarters to refrain from language stressing racial segregation. According to the account, both parties dropped the issue, and the general later told Adams that he had come to respect her.

Major Charity Adams Earley inspects the members of the 6888th Central Postal Directory Battalion on February 15, 1945, in Birmingham, England.

BLACK AND WHITE IN THE MILITARY

African Americans served in the military throughout American history, but they were relegated to segregated units. That policy did not change until after World War II, in 1948, when President Harry S. Truman signed Executive Order 9981 officially ending segregation in the military. Although the order was in place, the last all-black army unit wasn't disbanded until 1954.

In January 1941, the Army Nurse Corps changed its enlistment practices, allowing black women to join the army as nurses. They were given separate training and inferior living quarters and rations. (Susie King Taylor was an African American who served as a nurse during the Civil War, but she was never paid for her service.) Like the men, female recruits did not serve in integrated units until after 1948.

The navy didn't enlist women of color until 1945. The first black woman sworn into the navy was Phyllis Mae Dailey, a nurse and Columbia University student. She was the first of four African American women to serve in the navy during World War II. The other three were Edith Mazie Devoe, of Washington, DC; Helen Fredericka Turner, of Augusta, Georgia; and Eula Loucille Stimley, of Centreville, Mississippi.

father was a minister and her mother taught school. Charity graduated as valedictorian of her high school class and attended Wilberforce University, the first college owned and operated by African Americans. After graduation, she taught math in a segregated high school.

In July 1942, Adams enlisted in the Women's Army Auxiliary Corps and became the first African American woman to be an officer in the WAAC. The army was segregated, so she was placed in a company with other African American women.

Adams was dedicated and hardworking. She rose through the ranks, and in 1944 was appointed commanding officer of the 6888th Central Postal Directory Battalion, the first group of African American women serving overseas, first in Birmingham, England, then in France. In that position, Major Adams managed 850 women, who delivered mail to seven million soldiers.

After she completed her service, Adams went on to earn a master's degree in psychology from the Ohio State University, and then worked at the Veterans Administration in Cleveland. In 1949, she married Stanley A. Earley, Jr., and after a brief time overseas, they settled in Dayton, Ohio.

Major Earley did not appreciate the significance of the role she played in breaking down racial barriers at the time she was serving in the military. In 1996, the Smithsonian's National Postal Museum honored her for her wartime service. At the event she said, "When I talk to students, they say, 'How did it feel to know you were making history?' But you don't know you're making history when it's happening. I just wanted to do my job."

In her later career, Major Earley served on the board of directors of several civic and charitable organizations, including the American Red Cross and Sinclair Community College. She died in Dayton, Ohio, at age eighty-three on January 13, 2002.

On March 8, 1945, Phyllis Mae Dailey was sworn in as a member of the Navy Nurse Corps.

ANNIE G. FOX:
COOL UNDER FIRE

On December 7, 1941—the day the Japanese bombed Pearl Harbor—First Lieutenant Annie G. Fox calmly tended her patients while bombs exploded around her. Shaken by blasts and sickened by the black smoke darkening the sky, Fox, the chief nurse at the thirty-bed hospital on base at Pearl Harbor, continued to do her best to treat the injured soldiers, one at a time.

ANNIE G. FOX

Casualties poured into the hospital after the first wave of bombing. Lieutenant Fox and the six nurses working for her rushed into action, despite the sounds of bombs and machine gun and antiaircraft gunfire all around them. One bomb almost hit the hospital; it left a thirty-foot crater in the ground only steps away from the building. At one point, the smoke became so thick that the hospital staff had to put on gas masks because they worried they were experiencing a gas attack.

They didn't have enough nurses and doctors on call, so they had to make do with those who were available. During the emergency, Fox acted as a surgical assistant, administering anesthesia to patients during operations when there were no other doctors to help. She had no official training, but she followed the doctor's instructions as he told her what to do.

For her heroic service, forty-nine-year-old Fox was awarded the Purple Heart. She was the first woman to be given the honor. While typically bestowed upon soldiers wounded in

Lieutenant Annie G. Fox was the first woman to receive the Purple Heart for her service during the December 7, 1941, attack on Pearl Harbor.

"A DATE WHICH WILL LIVE IN INFAMY"

On December 7, 1941—a day President Franklin D. Roosevelt called "a date which will live in infamy"—the naval base at Pearl Harbor in Hawaii was attacked by more than 350 Japanese fighter planes. Following the attack, the United States entered World War II.

In the Battle of Pearl Harbor, more than 2,400 Americans were killed and almost 1,200 more were wounded. The attack damaged or destroyed nearly 300 U.S. aircraft, as well as twenty naval vessels, including eight battleships and three destroyers. The Japanese had aimed to destroy the entire American Pacific Fleet so that the United States could not respond as Japan pushed its armed forces across the South Pacific.

action, it could also be given for any "singularly meritorious act of extraordinary fidelity or essential service." Fox was recognized for her courage and leadership throughout the ordeal.

The military changed the criteria for the award in 1942, establishing that it should be

limited to those wounded as a result of enemy action. Lieutenant Fox had not been injured in the attack on Pearl Harbor, so she was asked to return the Purple Heart. On October 6, 1944, she was awarded the Bronze Star Medal in its place.

Lieutenant Fox had initially joined the Army Nurse Corps in 1918 at the end of World War I. She retired in 1945 after twenty-seven years of service. She died on January 20, 1987, at the age of ninety-three.

At about 8 a.m. hundreds of attack planes filled the sky, and the USS *Shaw* exploded during the Japanese raid on Pearl Harbor.

JOY BRIGHT HANCOCK:
RIDING THE WAVES

JOY BRIGHT HANCOCK

During her career, Captain Joy Bright Hancock witnessed dramatic changes in the opportunities open to women in the military. She served in both World War I and World War II, and she became director of the navy's WAVES.

Joy Bright was born on May 4, 1898, in Wildwood, New Jersey. She said that she was named Joy to offset her father's disappointment that his third child was not a boy. After attending business school, she enlisted in the navy as a yeoman (F), working in Camden, New Jersey, and at a naval air station in Wildwood during World War I. She quickly rose from yeoman (F) first class to chief yeoman.

After the war, Joy hoped to marry and start a family. She married navy pilot Lieutenant

Charles Gray Little, but in 1921 he was killed in the crash of an airship (also known as a zeppelin, dirigible, or blimp). The heartbroken widow took a job at the Bureau of Aeronautics, editing a newsletter, which later became the magazine *Naval Aviation News*. In 1924, she married another navy pilot, Lieutenant Commander Lewis Hancock, Jr. He also died in an airship accident the following year, leaving twenty-seven-year-old Joy a widow for the second time.

Instead of being frightened by air travel, Joy decided to face her fears and learn to fly. "I was afraid of anything that flew.... I reasoned that if I learned to fly, I might conquer my fear of it," she wrote in her 1972 autobiography, *Lady in the Navy: A Personal Reminiscence*. "The remedy worked."

In addition to flying, she loved learning how engines worked, and she spent a lot of time taking airplane engines apart and putting them together. She worked in the public relations office of the Bureau of Aeronautics.

When World War II began, Joy was commissioned as a lieutenant and joined the WAVES. She advocated for women's equality within the military, and by 1946, she had been promoted to the rank of captain and the position of director of WAVES. Her promotion was one of the fastest in the history of the navy.

In her position as director of WAVES, she testified before the Senate in favor of allowing women to be permanent members of the armed services. "It would appear to me that any national defense weapon known to be of value should be developed and kept in good working order and not allowed to rust or to be abolished," she said. The Women's Armed Services Integration Act, which she helped write, passed Congress and was signed by President Truman in 1948.

Captain Hancock retired from active duty in June 1953. The following year she married Vice Admiral Ralph A. Ofstie, but he died several years later. She lived in the Washington, DC, area. She died on August 20, 1986, at age eighty-eight.

OVETA CULP HOBBY:
SETTING A NEW DIRECTION

During World War II, the United States Army needed the Women's Army Corps, and the Women's Army Corps needed Colonel Oveta Culp Hobby. During her military career, Colonel Hobby headed the War Department's Women's Interest Section, served as the director of the Women's Army Auxiliary Corps, and became the first director of the Women's Army Corps.

Oveta Culp was a thoughtful and intelligent child. She was born on January 19, 1905, in Killeen, Texas, and even as a young girl, she was a serious thinker. When she was six years old, an anti-alcohol group asked her to sign a pledge that she would never drink liquor. She thought about it and refused; she explained that at that point in her life she had no intention of ever drinking alcohol, but she did not know if she might someday change her mind, and she didn't want to make a promise she wasn't sure she would keep.

OVETA CULP HOBBY

She was also a serious reader. At age ten, she began reading the *Congressional Record*. As a teen, she read the Bible cover to cover three times.

Oveta attended Mary Hardin Baylor College for Women and the South Texas College of Law and Commerce, but she didn't graduate from either school. She studied law at the University of Texas Law School, but she did not formally enroll in the program, so she did not receive a degree. Her father served in the Texas House of Representatives; and as a teenager, she spent a lot of time watching him in chambers, so she became very familiar with how things were done. When she was twenty-one, she worked for the Texas House of Representatives as the expert in rules and procedures.

Later Oveta had a career in journalism working at the *Houston Post*, rising through the ranks and eventually becoming publisher. In 1931, she married William Hobby, the former governor of Texas and a close friend of her father's. She was twenty-six years old; he was fifty-three.

Oveta served on several state boards and commissions, where she demonstrated a skill at organizing large groups. When World War II began, she was contacted by an army general who asked her to help coordinate female volunteers within the military. At the time, the War Department was receiving 10,000 letters a day from women who wanted to support the war effort.

Although she was reluctant to serve at first, with the encouragement of her husband, Oveta finally agreed to become director of the Women's Army Auxiliary Corps. In 1943, the WAAC was converted into the Women's Army Corps, a part of the regular army. She oversaw the introduction of women in the armed forces, as well as their service overseas. She was promoted to the rank of colonel, and she received the Distinguished Service Medal, becoming the first woman in the army to receive this honor. She also received honorary degrees from seventeen colleges and universities, including Columbia University.

After the war, Colonel Hobby worked in radio and TV, and she returned to the *Houston Post*. She was also appointed to a number of jobs by political allies, and she served on various boards of directors. In 1953, she became the first secretary of the Department of Health, Education, and Welfare, which later became the Department of Health and Human

WOMEN'S WORK

Under Colonel Hobby's direction, the jobs open to women in the military expanded. Evidence showed that women could perform most jobs just as well as men, and there were some tasks, such as secretarial work and parachute folding, where women were faster and more efficient than men.

In 1941, Congress established the Women's Army Auxiliary Corps, which worked with the army "for the purpose of making available to the national defense the knowledge, skill, and special training of the women of the nation." Women served in nonfighting roles. "The gaps our women will fill are in those noncombatant jobs where women's hands and women's hearts fit naturally," Colonel Hobby said. "WAACs will do the same type of work which women do in civilian life."

Two years later, the WAAC was converted into the Women's Army Corps, which made women a part of the regular army. This was an important step forward because the army could offer greater protection to women if they were considered members of the military, and women could qualify for more benefits.

Colonel Oveta Hobby expanded the role of women in the army. In the early days of the Women's Army Corps, women were authorized to perform only fifty-four jobs; when Colonel Hobby left her post, women had been cleared to fill 239 different job categories. They were no longer just typists and stenographers and drivers, but aerial photograph analysts, control tower operators, and ordnance engineers. More than 150,000 American women served in the Women's Army Corps during World War II.

Services. In this position, she once again helped to organize a large government agency. One of her most notable achievements in that office was the approval of the Salk polio vaccine.

Colonel Hobby died of a stroke on August 16, 1995, at the age of ninety, and was buried in Houston.

GRACE HOPPER:
"AMAZING GRACE"

GRACE HOPPER

Grace Hopper was a brilliant mathematician who put her talent to work programming computers for the military. One of her most important contributions was the invention of a computer programming language based on English words. This revolutionary idea became the foundation of a programming language that is still used today.

Grace Brewster Murray was born on December 9, 1906, in New York City. As a child, she was very bright and curious. When she was seven years old, she wanted to understand how alarm clocks worked, so she took apart not one but all seven clocks in the house. At age sixteen, she applied to Vassar College but was denied admission because her scores in Latin were too low. She tried again the next year and got in, graduating Phi Beta Kappa with degrees in physics and mathematics. She went on to receive a PhD in mathematics from Yale University. She became a professor at Vassar College and married New York University professor Vincent Foster Hopper in 1930; they were divorced in 1945.

When World War II broke out, Grace Hopper tried to enlist in the navy, but was turned away. At age thirty-four, she was considered too old. Instead she got a leave of absence from Vassar and joined the navy WAVES, but she had to get a waiver because she was fifteen pounds underweight. The navy overlooked her age and weight because they recognized

Captain Grace Hopper in 1976, at that time the head of the Navy Programming Language Section of the Chief of Naval Operations.

that she would be a great help in the development of computers for use in the military.

Hopper trained at and graduated from the Naval Reserve Midshipmen's School at Smith College. She was sworn in as a lieutenant, junior grade, and was assigned as a military expert to work at Harvard University, where she became the third programmer of the Mark I, the world's first large-scale computer. She stayed in that position until 1949, turning down the chance to become a full professor at Vassar.

In 1949, she helped design the first commercial computer, which was known as UNIVAC I (UNIVersal Automatic Computer I). When Hopper suggested that the team work on a programming language that would use English words, her colleagues told her that computers didn't understand English. She knew that they could if they were programmed properly, and she went to work. Three years later in 1952 she completed a compiler, which could translate one computer program into another. This became the foundation of the computer program COBOL (Common Business-Oriented Language).

In 1966, Hopper retired from the Naval Reserve. The following year, the navy recalled her to active duty because the other programmers needed her help standardizing communication between different computer languages. She was promoted to captain in 1973 and commodore in 1983. (In 1985 the rank of commodore was renamed rear admiral.)

When she finally retired in 1986, she was almost eighty years old—the oldest active-duty commissioned officer in the navy.

Her revolutionary work in computer science earned her the nickname Amazing Grace. She was also awarded the Defense Distinguished Service Medal, the National Medal of Technology, and forty honorary degrees from universities around the world. President

Barack Obama posthumously awarded her the Presidential Medal of Freedom in 2016. A supercomputer and a guided-missile destroyer were named in her honor.

Hopper died on January 1, 1992, in Arlington, Virginia, at age eighty-five.

THE USS *HOPPER*

The USS *Hopper* is a guided missile destroyer in the navy named for computer scientist Commodore Grace Hopper. The USS *Hopper* was launched in 1996. The ship's motto is Dare and Do. It is only the second navy warship named for a woman who served in the navy. (The first was the USS *Higbee*, named for Lenah S. Higbee, superintendent of the Navy Nurse Corps during World War I; see page 58.)

The names of commissioned ships of the United States Navy start with USS, which stands for United States ship. The secretary of the navy chooses the names of the ships, usually in honor of states, towns, people, battles, or ideas.

The USS *Hopper* leaving Honolulu, Hawaii

ALEDA E. LUTZ:
FEARLESS IN FLIGHT

ALEDA E. LUTZ

Again and again and again, First Lieutenant Aleda E. Lutz put her life at risk to save others. As a volunteer with the 802nd Medical Air Evacuation Transport Squadron, Lutz flew 196 missions—814 hours—and helped to evacuate more than 3,500 soldiers during World War II. No other flight nurse came close to logging as many hours in the air as Lutz, and not a single one of the patients she treated in flight died while in her care.

Unfortunately, on November 1, 1944, her luck ran out. While transporting fifteen wounded soldiers—nine Americans and six German prisoners of war—from France to Italy, the C-47 she was flying in crashed into the side of Mont Pelat, the highest mountain in the Mercantour National Park in France. It is unclear if the pilot lost his bearings during a violent storm or if enemy forces shot down the plane. No one survived. Lutz was the only woman on board, and she became the first American woman killed in action during World War II.

Lutz was born on November 9, 1915, in Freeland, Michigan. Her parents were immigrants from Nuremberg, Germany, and she grew up speaking both English and German. Lutz, the youngest of ten children, graduated from the Saginaw General Hospital School of Nursing in 1937. She worked at the Saginaw General Hospital until the beginning of World War II.

In 1942, she enlisted in the Army Nurse Corps, and was commissioned as a second lieutenant. She was a general duty nurse in Mount Clemens, Michigan, before transferring to the 349th Air Evacuation Camp. This assignment was an honor: only about 2 percent of the nurses who served in World War II qualified as flight nurses. Lutz was then promoted to first lieutenant and reassigned to the 802nd Medical Air Evacuation Transport Squadron in 1943. She worked tirelessly; once she went out on four different missions in a single day. She also accepted dangerous assignments; her squadron went deep into combat zones in France, Italy, and Tunisia.

Lutz was the first woman to be awarded the Distinguished Flying Cross. She also received the Air Medal, the Red Cross Medal, six battle stars, and the Purple Heart. She received all of these honors in only twenty months of service! Aleda Lutz was twenty-eight years old when she died. She is buried in France. In 1945, an 800-patient hospital ship was renamed in honor of her. A Veterans Affairs Medical Center in Saginaw, Michigan, was also named in her honor in recognition of her courageous service during World War II.

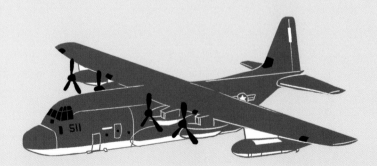

ELSIE OTT:
BRINGING NURSING TO THE SKIES

Elsie Ott had never been on a plane, but that didn't stop her from accepting an assignment that would revolutionize the way the military ran air rescue operations. In an experimental mission in 1941, Ott helped rescue five seriously ill patients, caring for them as they were airlifted from India to the United States. She then helped to establish the army's air evacuation program, which would dramatically improve survival rates for soldiers serving on the front lines.

Ott was born in Smithtown, New York, on November 5, 1913. She attended Lenox Hill Hospital School of Nursing in New York City and joined the United States Army Air Force Nurse Corps in 1941, serving as a second lieu-

ELSIE OTT

tenant. In the early days of World War II, there were no air ambulances. While some patients had been airlifted out of certain places in Alaska, New Guinea, and other remote areas, the military did not have an organized method of moving injured soldiers by air. That changed when Ott was stationed as a nurse with the First Troop Carrier Command in Karachi, India, and she was asked to participate in a test of the first intercontinental medical air transport team.

Ott volunteered to serve as the only nurse on the inaugural flight. She had less than twenty-four hours to prepare a D-47 Air Transport Command plane, converting it into a mobile hospital. She only had basic items that might be found in a first aid kit. She stocked the plane with blankets, bandages, and other supplies she thought her patients might need.

The mission came with considerable risk: since the plane was carrying troops, it could not bear the Red Cross insignia, indicating that it was a strictly humanitarian mission. As a result, the plane was a target that could be struck down by enemy fire.

On January 17, 1943, the experiment began. The medical evacuation plane brought combat troops to the front lines and carried out five patients. Ott's first job was to evaluate the injuries and stabilize the patients. The needs of the patients were varied: two were paralyzed from the waist down, one had tuberculosis, one had glaucoma, and a fifth had suffered a nervous breakdown.

The plane had a brief layover partway back to the United States so that the patients

Brigadier General Fred W. Borum presents the Air Medal
to Second Lieutenant Elsie Ott.

could be seen by physicians and additional patients could board. After a difficult flight, the plane finally landed at Morrison Field in Florida, then went on to Walter Reed Hospital in Washington, DC. The six-day, 11,000-mile trip by air would have taken at least three months by ship and ground transportation.

Based on her experience, Ott offered recommendations on how the army could implement an air evacuation program. In part, she recommended that flights be equipped with oxygen and sufficient bandages, and that nurses be permitted to wear pants, rather than skirts.

Her work proved that air evacuation was not only possible but preferable to ground transportation in many cases, since the injured could be moved more quickly to better-equipped hospitals. The army created a flight evacuation school at Bowman Army Air Field in Kentucky. Ott asked to attend the training program; she was trained and became part of the 803rd Medical Air Evacuation Transport Squadron.

In recognition of her work, in 1943 Ott became the first woman to receive the army's Air Medal. She was promoted to captain and served in the army until her discharge in 1946. She then married and settled in Wheaton, Illinois. She died in 2006 at the age of ninety-three.

AIR AMBULANCES

Before World War II, air evacuation was considered too dangerous and too expensive to be effective. That changed in 1942, when the Army Air Corps established medical air evacuation squadrons to help transport injured soldiers from the battlefield to medical facilities.

Air evacuation improved survival rates of wounded soldiers. Of the nearly 1.2 million patients evacuated by air during World War II, only forty-six died en route. These were dangerous missions, however. Of the 500 flight nurses who served on air evacuation squadrons, seventeen were killed during their service. Today air evacuation, typically by helicopter, has become commonplace.

THE FLIGHT NURSE'S CREED

I will summon every resource to prevent the triumph of death over life.

I will stand guard over the medicines and equipment entrusted to my care and ensure their proper use.

I will be untiring in the performances of my duties and I will remember that, upon my disposition and spirit, will in large measure depend the morale of my patients.

I will be faithful to my training and to the wisdom handed down to me by those who have gone before me.

I have taken a nurse's oath, reverent in man's mind because of the spirit and work of its creator, Florence Nightingale. She, I remember, was called the "Lady with the Lamp."

It is now my privilege to lift this lamp of hope and faith and courage in my profession to heights not known by her in her time. Together with the help of flight surgeons and surgical technicians, I can set the very skies ablaze with life and promise for the sick, injured, and wounded who are my sacred charges.

. . . This I will do. I will not falter in war or in peace.

The Flight Nurse's Creed was included in a speech given by the air surgeon of the United States Army Air Forces, Major General David N. W. Grant, on November 26, 1943.

CLAIRE PHILLIPS:
GENERAL MACARTHUR'S SPY

Claire Phillips never enlisted in the military, but she nobly served the United States. She wasn't who she appeared to be. To the Japanese officers who visited her nightclub, she was Dorothy Clara Fuentes, a singer, dancer, and club owner. To American general Douglas MacArthur, she was Claire Phillips, a spy who provided important information that helped the Allied forces in the Pacific during World War II.

Claire Phillips was born Claire Maybelle Snyder on December 2, 1907, in Michigan. As a young woman, she joined a musical company on tour in the Philippines. While overseas in 1941, she met and married John Phillips, an American soldier. He was captured by the Japanese and died in a prison camp. A soldier convinced Claire to join a spy ring and pass information to the Americans; she agreed, eager to avenge her husband's death.

Phillips took the name "Dorothy Clara Fuentes" and made up a story about her past as a Philippine-born Italian dancer. (She chose her history because she assumed that most Japanese military officers wouldn't know Italian so they wouldn't ask her many questions about her past.) Phillips and another dancer opened a nightclub in Manila known as the Tsubaki Club. The club, located near the harbor where the military ships docked, catered to Japanese soldiers: the performers sang Japanese songs and featured Japanese drinks.

Every night, Phillips danced for the officers and encouraged them to drink a lot of alcohol. She would flirt with them and try to get information. Sometimes she would have an employee pretend to take a photo of her with the officer, then ask for his address so she could send the picture to him. Using this approach, she would find out where the military was

> In addition to spying, Claire Phillips paid to have messages, medical supplies, and food smuggled to prisoners of war held in prison camps. She was called High Pockets because she often hid messages in her bra.

headed next. At the end of the evening, she would write a report of everything she and the other spies in her operation had learned, and she would send it to General MacArthur by messenger.

In 1944, one of the messengers was captured, and Phillips's identity was revealed. She was arrested and taken to a prisoner of war camp. She spent nine months being tortured, but she did not reveal any names or information about the spy ring. In 1945, American troops liberated Phillips from the camp. She had lost fifty-five pounds and was near death from starvation.

In 1951, she was awarded the Medal of Freedom on the recommendation of General MacArthur. Phillips died of alcoholism-related meningitis at age fifty-two on May 22, 1960, in Portland, Oregon.

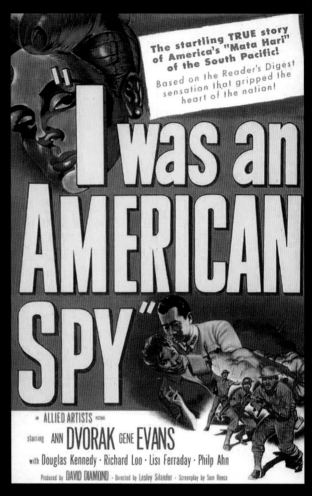

In 1947, Claire Phillips released her memoir, *Manila Espionage*, cowritten by Myron B. Goldsmith. The book was adapted into the 1951 movie *I Was an American Spy*.

REBA Z. WHITTLE:
THE SILENT PRISONER OF WAR

REBA Z. WHITTLE

On September 27, 1944, Second Lieutenant Reba Z. Whittle looked out of the C-47 she was flying in and saw one engine in flames after being hit by enemy fire. The plane crashed, and the survivors crawled from the burning wreckage, only to be immediately captured by German soldiers. Whittle was grateful to be alive but terrified to be held captive. She became the only female prisoner of war in Europe during World War II.

Reba Zitella Whittle was born August 19, 1919, in Rocksprings, Texas. She studied at North Texas State College and the Medical and Surgical Memorial Hospital School of Nursing in San Antonio. In 1942, she enlisted in the U.S. Army Nurse Corps as a second lieutenant. She almost didn't make the cut: At five feet, seven inches tall, she weighed just 117 pounds, seven

First Lieutenant Reba Z. Whittle never discussed her experiences as a prisoner of war with her two sons, one of whom served in the military during the Vietnam War.

pounds below the weight minimum. The recruiter allowed her to join but encouraged her to put on a little weight.

Whittle served in hospitals in Albuquerque, New Mexico, and Sacramento, California, then began training as a flight nurse at the Bowman Army Air Field in Kentucky. Several weeks after completing the six-week training, she flew to England to join the 813th Medical Air Evacuation Transport Squadron.

Whittle flew on forty missions and logged more than 500 hours of flight time between January and September 1944, when her plane was shot down. After they were captured, the surviving crew members were taken to a nearby village and treated for their injuries before being moved to a hospital. Because she was the only female prisoner of war, the Germans weren't sure how to handle her. She was taken to a military hospital where she worked taking care of burn patients and amputees until the military negotiated for her release. She returned to the United States on January 25, 1945.

When Whittle got home, she was asked to sign an agreement with the military that read, in part: "I understand that all information concerning escape, evasion from capture . . . and details of imprisonment or release from internment, is SECRET and must not be disclosed. . . . I realize that publicity concerning my experiences . . . will endanger the lives of many persons and therefore it is my duty to take all possible precautions to prevent it." She never discussed her capture or wartime experiences, even with her family.

Whittle was recognized for her wartime service. In 1945, she was awarded the Purple Heart and the Air Medal, and she was promoted to first lieutenant. Later that summer, she married Lieutenant Colonel Stanley W. Tobiason. She asked to be released from active duty and was discharged from the military in January 1946.

Unfortunately, Whittle was unable to put her wartime trauma behind her. She suffered from physical and psychiatric problems, including post-traumatic stress disorder. She had to argue with the military to receive disability compensation and retirement pay benefits.

Whittle died of cancer in Sacramento, California, on January 26, 1981, at the age of sixty-one.

FRANCES WILLS, HARRIET PICKENS,
AND MILDRED MCAFEE: THREE WHO DARED

Lieutenant (junior grade) Harriet Ida Pickens and Ensign Frances Wills
on December 21, 1944, the day they graduated from the Naval Reserve
Midshipmen's School

They may not have realized the full importance of what they were doing at the time, but three women revolutionized the way things were done in the United States Navy. On December 21, 1944, Frances Wills and Harriet Pickens became the first African American women to be commissioned as naval officers; as the director of the navy's program for women, Mildred H. McAfee pushed to open the military to women, regardless of the color of their skin.

Wills and Pickens were well qualified for their groundbreaking positions. Frances Eliza Wills was born in Philadelphia in 1916 and raised in New York. She graduated from Hunter

College and worked with renowned African American poet Langston Hughes while getting her master's degree in social work from the University of Pittsburgh.

Harriet Ida Pickens was born in 1909, the daughter of William Pickens, one of the founders of the National Association for the Advancement of Colored People. She graduated from Smith College, then received a master's degree in political science from Columbia University.

They had outstanding qualifications and were ready to enlist when the Naval Reserve Midshipmen's School (Women's Reserve) at Smith College in Northampton, Massachusetts, finally admitted African American women. Both Wills and Pickens were at an immediate disadvantage compared to their classmates. The navy did not decide to integrate the program until mid-October, a month behind the other officer candidates. But both women worked to catch up and rose to the top of the class by the time they graduated in December.

The opportunity offered to Wills and Pickens was the result of navy captain Mildred H.

Lieutenant Commander Mildred McAfee Horton (1900–1994) was the first director of WAVES. She was the first woman to receive the Navy Distinguished Service Medal.

McAfee's tireless efforts to integrate the navy. McAfee—the former president of Wellesley College—served as the first director of the WAVES. She had been hired to organize the WAVES program, and Mc-Afee insisted on opening the program to African Americans.

In August 1942, McAfee also became one of the navy's first female commissioned officers when she became a lieutenant commander in the Naval Reserve. In 1943, she was promoted to captain. McAfee believed that African American women should have equal rights to participate in the military. At the time, all of the armed forces were segregated. Under pressure from a number of civil rights organizations, earlier in 1944 the navy had finally agreed to commission the first male African American officers for all African American units.

Secretary of the Navy Frank Knox told McAfee that African American women would enlist in the WAVES over his dead body. He was right: he died in office in 1944 and was replaced by the more forward-thinking secretary James Forrestal, who accepted integration. At the time, there weren't enough African American women applying for the WAVES to outfit an entire unit, so the plan for integration moved forward. By the end of the war, seventy-two African American women had joined the WAVES.

In 1945, McAfee married Rev. Dr. Douglas Horton, the dean of the divinity school at Harvard University. She left the military in 1946 and returned to her position as president of Wellesley College. She died from breast cancer in 1994. Wills died in 1998; Pickens died in 1969.

HERE TO STAY:

WOMEN IN THE KOREAN WAR

During World War II, women proved their importance to the nation's military. More than 350,000 women served their country honorably, and their contributions—as nurses, pilots, engineers, and in almost every other noncombat job—helped to ensure the victory of the Allied forces.

After the war, all the branches of the armed forces had to reevaluate the role of women in the military. Initially, women were expected to serve for the duration of the war, plus six months. But the use of women in the military had proved so successful that there was a movement to make women a permanent part of the armed forces. And in 1948, Congress passed the Women's Armed Services Integration Act, which gave women permanent status and granted them veterans' benefits.

In the postwar period, Congress also established the air force as a separate branch of the armed services. Some women who had served with the air force in the Women's Army Corps (WAC) decided to transfer to Women in the Air Force (WAF), the women's unit of the new air force. (The WAF remained active until 1976, when women were finally accepted into the air

THE KOREAN WAR (1950–1953)

The Korean War was fought between North Korea (with support from the Soviet Union and China) and South Korea (with support from the United States). The United States supplied most of the soldiers, but other countries contributed troops. Korea had been ruled by Japan from 1910 until the end of World War II. In 1948 Korea split into two regions along the Thirty-Eighth parallel with separate governments, but neither side accepted the status of the other. The fighting began in 1950 when North Korea invaded South Korea. The fighting stopped in 1953, but no peace treaty was ever signed.

force on an equal basis with men.) At first, Women in the Air Force was limited to 4,000 enlisted women and 300 female officers. Although they worked for the air force, women were not trained or permitted to serve as pilots; most served in clerical or medical positions.

Social trends after World War II reestablished the feminine ideals of woman as wife, mother, and homemaker. Many women readily embraced these traditional roles, but some didn't want to give up the independence and self-worth they had discovered in military service and work outside the home. Women who wanted to serve in the military had to choose between service and family: a woman would be discharged if she became pregnant, and mothers with children under age eighteen were not allowed to enlist. Despite these restrictions, many women did continue with their military service.

Not long after the new organization of the military, the United States was drawn back into war. In 1950, President Harry Truman ordered the armed forces into combat in Korea. During the Korean War, more than 50,000 women served at home and abroad.

One of the most important changes in military organization was the creation of MASH units (Mobile Army Surgical Hospitals) in combat zones. More than 700 women served as nurses in MASH units, which were credited with lowering death rates from battle injuries by 50 percent, compared to World War II levels. In addition, helicopters were introduced, allowing for speedier evacuation of the wounded and making it easier to move troops and supplies.

Army women who had joined the reserves following World War II were involuntarily recalled to active duty during the Korean War. Although no Women's Army Corps units were sent to Korea, about a dozen WACs served in Korea in administrative roles.

During the Korean War, medical air evacuation nurses and medical specialists were the only women in the air force allowed to serve in the battle zone. Other women served in support roles as air traffic controllers, weather observers, parachute riggers, and radar operators.

STAFF SERGEANT BARBARA BARNWELL:
COURAGE AT SEA

Staff Sergeant
Barbara Barnwell

She may not have been fighting against an armed enemy, but the United States Marine Corps recognized that Sergeant Barbara Barnwell risked her life to save a fellow marine. On June 7, 1952, Barnwell was swimming in the Atlantic Ocean near Marine Corps Camp Lejeune, North Carolina. She heard cries from someone struggling in the surf. She immediately swam toward Marine Private Frederick H. Roman, who was caught in an undertow and fighting against the powerful current.

When Barnwell reached the drowning soldier, she put her arms around him. He scratched and clung to her, pushing her under the water several times, but Barnwell persisted in her attempt to pull him toward land. It took twenty minutes for Barnhill to swim the 120 yards to shore. When she reached shallow water, a lifeguard helped her carry Roman, who was unconscious, up to the beach.

Stories of the heroic rescue spread, and Barnwell was recognized for her selfless heroism. On August 7, 1953, she was awarded the Navy and Marine Corps Medal for heroism, the first woman to receive the honor.

It wasn't the first time Barnwell had saved someone who was drowning. When she was just eleven years old, Barnwell had rescued a seven-year-old child from drowning in Kansas City.

Barbara Olive Barnwell was born in 1928 in Kansas City, Missouri. She enlisted in the Marine Corps in May 1949 and served as a naval gunfire instructor with the First Air and Naval Gunfire Liaison Company at the time of the rescue. She died at age forty-nine in Santa Barbara, California, in April 1977.

ESTHER BLAKE:
FIRST IN LINE

In March 1944, Esther Blake, a forty-seven-year-old widow, learned that her son, Lieutenant Julius Blake, was missing in action after his B-17 was shot down over Belgium. She wanted to do everything in her power to support the war effort and secure her son's safe return, so she joined the Women's Army Corps. It was not long before she was notified that her second son, Lieutenant Tom Blake, had also been shot down while flying a bomber over Italy. She continued her work with the corps, doubling her dedication to the cause.

ESTHER BLAKE

Fortunately, both sons eventually returned home safely. Blake was discharged at the end of World War II, but she remained dedicated to the military. When she learned that the air force was going to begin accepting women for peacetime service, she knew she wanted to serve.

On July 8, 1948, she was ready: Blake made an effort to be the first to enlist on the day that the air force accepted women. She retired from the air force in 1954 and worked for the Veterans Administration until her death in Tuskegee, Alabama, on October 17, 1979, at age eighty-two.

JONITA RUTH BONHAM:
"THE NURSE WHO FORGOT FEAR"

JONITA RUTH
BONHAM

Jonita Ruth Bonham served as a flight nurse with the 801st Medical Air Evacuation Squadron in Tachikawa, Japan, during the Korean War. Before serving in the Korean War, Bonham had volunteered as a second lieutenant in the Medical Corps of the Army Air Corps during World War II. After the war, she resigned from active duty, but rejoined the military to serve in the Korean War as a first lieutenant in the air force.

On the night of September 26, 1950, she was flying on a C-54 cargo plane that had been converted to a mobile emergency hospital. About a half mile from shore, the plane stalled and crashed into the Sea of Japan.

The aircraft broke into three pieces and began to sink. Bonham fought her way out of

the submerged plane and began swimming through the choppy seas. She clung to a floating bag until she could reach a rope tied to a life raft. Rather than climbing to safety, Bonham stayed in the water and pulled other survivors toward the boat. She didn't seem to take account of her own injuries; she rescued seventeen of her patients before finally being pulled onto one of two life rafts.

The survivors were found by a Japanese fishing boat and taken to shore. Bonham spent nine months in the hospital recovering from her injuries, which included a fractured skull and broken bones in her face, shoulder, and wrist.

In recognition of her selfless and heroic efforts to save her patients, on October 18, 1950, in Tokyo, General George Stratemeyer gave Bonham the Distinguished Flying Cross, making her the first female recipient of this honor. The *Cavalcade of America* radio show aired a program about her titled "The Nurse Who Forgot Fear" on April 9, 1952. Articles about her bravery appeared in *Reader's Digest* and various women's magazines. She was promoted to captain, and remained in the military for two years after the accident. She married Colonel Clifton Willard Bovee, and they had three children. She retired from the military for medical reasons in 1952.

Bonham died of cancer in Colorado Springs, Colorado, on December 24, 1994, at age seventy-two.

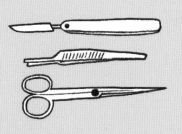

ELEANOR C. L'ECUYER:
REDEFINING THE ROLE OF WOMEN

ELEANOR C. L'ECUYER

When Eleanor C. L'Ecuyer left the Coast Guard Reserve, she didn't expect to reenlist. And she never imagined that she would play a role in challenging military policies that were unfair to women.

L'Ecuyer was born in Boston, Massachusetts, on June 13, 1922. During World War II, she served in the SPARs, the female branch of the Coast Guard Reserve. She worked in the pharmacy department at the Coast Guard Air Station Port Angeles in Washington until her discharge in 1946. After she left the service, she enrolled at Suffolk University in Boston on the GI Bill, which offered assistance to soldiers returning from military service. L'Ecuyer graduated with a law degree in 1950.

At the time, there weren't many jobs for female lawyers. L'Ecuyer saw a newspaper ad encouraging coast guard veterans who had received specialty training in the postwar years to return to the military. When L'Ecuyer applied, she was told that the opportunity was only for men who had served. She argued her case and was allowed to take the necessary entrance exams. "They let me take the test anyway, thinking I'd fail," she said.

But she cleared every hurdle. On the same day she found out she had passed the test, she also learned she had passed the Massachusetts Bar.

L'Ecuyer rejoined the military as a lieutenant junior grade in the Coast Guard Women's Reserve. She became the first female attorney hired by the coast guard, although she did not serve in the military as a lawyer.

During her time in the coast guard, L'Ecuyer used her legal training to test several coast guard policies that were unfair to women. She challenged the idea that pregnancy was a disabling condition that required discharge from the military. She also pushed back against policies that prevented married couples from relocating together, and those that limited women to twenty years of military service. These policy changes increased the career potential for women in the coast guard.

L'Ecuyer was promoted to captain and served until 1971. In addition to being the first female lawyer in the coast guard, L'Ecuyer holds the distinction of being the longest-serving SPAR.

GERALDINE PRATT MAY:
ORGANIZING THE AIR FORCE

GERALDINE PRATT MAY

On June 12, 1948, President Harry Truman signed the Women's Armed Services Integration Act, giving women the right to serve as permanent members of the armed forces. What would that new law mean to women who wanted to serve in the air force? Colonel Geraldine Pratt May helped to answer that question when she became the first director of Women in the Air Force four days later.

May was born in Albany, New York, on April 21, 1895, and graduated from the University of California at Berkeley. She had a job as a social worker and as an executive with the Camp Fire Girls before joining the Women's Army Auxiliary Corps in 1942, after her husband was killed in the war. May entered the first class of officer candidates. She was forty-seven

years old when she enlisted—two years beyond the age limit—but an exception was made to allow her to join the military because of her education and work experience.

Initially, May accepted an assignment with the Army Air Forces because the air force was not yet a separate branch of the military. She served as staff director of the Air Transport Command, overseeing 6,000 enlisted women and officers. Her outstanding service during the war made her an ideal candidate to serve as director of Women in the Air Force when that program was established in 1949.

In addition to taking on the responsibilities as director, fifty-five-year-old May was also promoted to colonel, becoming the first woman in the air force to earn that rank. As director, May visited air bases around the world and helped create policies involved in bringing women into the regular and reserve air force. The first women who served wore men's uniforms with neckties; May lobbied to change the dress code so that women could wear uniforms that were more feminine and comfortable, like those worn by airline stewardesses.

She wanted to make women the equal of men in the air force, but she felt frustrated when she met with a lot of resistance. Hers was an advisory role, meaning that air force leaders could accept or ignore her recommendations. Still, by advocating on behalf of women she forced men to at least consider the possibility of an air force with more females in leadership positions.

May earned the respect of her colleagues. "Her low-key demeanor disguised a strong will and an iron determination," wrote an officer who worked with her. She was "not given to compromise on matters of principle."

She served as director until 1951 when she retired from the military. She died on November 2, 1997, in Menlo Park, California, at age 102.

BREAKING THE BRASS CEILING:

WOMEN IN THE VIETNAM WAR

Not long after the Korean War ended in 1953, the United States became involved in a conflict in Vietnam. Ultimately, the dispute came to represent the battle over communism. The United States feared that if communist North Vietnam won the war, the result would be the spread of communism throughout the area.

As with all previous battles, women served in the Vietnam War. By the time America started sending military advisers into the area in 1955, women were involved in every branch of the armed forces, but, frankly, their roles were still very limited. Of the 11,000 women who served in Vietnam, 90 percent served as nurses. The others were air traffic controllers, intelligence officers, clerks, communications experts, weather monitors, and other support jobs. While women were accepted as an important part of the military, they served in a limited number of positions.

Every woman who served in Vietnam volunteered for service. That was not true of the men. For most of U.S. history, American males over age eighteen had been required to register with the federal government for the draft. If called on, they had to serve in the military.

THE VIETNAM WAR (1955–1975)

The Vietnam War was fought between North Vietnam (supported by the Soviet Union, China, and other communist countries) and South Vietnam (supported by the United States, Australia, and other anti-communist countries). It began in November 1955 and ended on April 30, 1975, when Saigon fell to the North Vietnamese. American leaders believed in the "domino theory," which argued that if one country in a region became communist, the surrounding countries would follow, like one domino knocking down another.

As the Vietnam War continued and the death toll rose, U.S. citizens became increasingly divided over their support for American involvement in the war and over the issue of the draft. Antiwar activists held protests and public demonstrations; many people turned against the war. In response, in 1973, Congress ended the draft, and the military became an all-volunteer force.

This change had a dramatic impact on women in the armed forces. Switching to an all-volunteer force meant that the military needed to create incentives for people to enlist. To lure prospective recruits, the military increased the base pay for soldiers and created more opportunities for women.

But now, even with the need for soldiers, there were still limits to what women were allowed to do in the military. As with previous wars, women were not allowed to serve in combat. That's not to say they didn't face significant personal risk: many female nurses worked in or near combat zones, and they had to deal with other dangers and difficulties of being in remote areas of foreign countries. In fact, eight women were killed in combat in Vietnam, even though they did not fight or carry weapons.

A WOMAN'S WORLD

During the 1960s and 1970s, the legal status of women changed in the United States. Step by step, women gained more legal protections in a number of areas.

- In 1964, Title VII of the Civil Rights Act outlawed sex discrimination in employment.
- In 1965, the Equal Employment Opportunity Commission was created.
- In 1965, Executive Order 11246 made it illegal for government contractors to discriminate on the basis of sex.
- In 1972, Title IX of the Education Amendments Act prohibited sex discrimination in educational programs, including girls' sports in public schools.
- In 1974, the Equal Credit Opportunity Act gave women the right to apply for credit without a male cosigner.
- In 1975, the U.S. Supreme Court ruled that it was illegal to exclude women from serving on juries.
- In 1978, the Pregnancy Discrimination Act made it illegal to fire a woman for being pregnant.

These laws helped to expand opportunities for women. At the same time, the military provided more chances for women to serve and to establish careers in the armed forces.

BREAKING THE BRASS CEILING

In some ways, the changes in the military reflected the changes taking place in civilian life during the Vietnam War years. The feminist movement and the civil rights movement were reshaping American life. New opportunities opened to women both in and out of the military. More jobs were available to women, and, for the first time, there was more chance for advancement so women could consider a career in the armed forces.

WOMEN AND THE DRAFT

Today, people volunteer to join the military, but at various points in history able-bodied men have been drafted (or conscripted), meaning they have been required to enlist and serve in the armed forces. The draft has been used five times in American history: during the Revolution, the Civil War, World War I, World War II, and the Cold War (which includes both the Korean War and the Vietnam War).

The draft is typically activated in times of war or national emergency. The first peacetime draft started in 1940, when soldiers were called on to fill open positions in the military. The practice continued until the draft was suspended in 1975. Although the military has switched to an all-volunteer force, the draft could be reactivated, if necessary. If the draft were reintroduced in the future, women would almost certainly be required to register and serve as well.

EIGHT ON THE WALL

Eight women died in combat during the Vietnam War and have their names engraved on the Vietnam Veterans Memorial, in Washington, DC. They are:

Captain Eleanor Grace Alexander

Second Lieutenant Pamela Dorothy Donovan

Second Lieutenant Carol Ann Elizabeth Drazba

Lieutenant Colonel Annie Ruth Graham

Second Lieutenant Elizabeth Ann Jones

Captain Mary Therese Klinker

First Lieutenant Sharon Ann Lane

First Lieutenant Hedwig Diane Orlowski

The two-acre Vietnam Veterans Memorial is a national monument that honors service members who fought and died in the Vietnam War. The wall was completed in 1982.

BARBARA J. DULINSKY:
VOLUNTEERING IN VIETNAM

BARBARA J. DULINSKY

On March 18, 1967, after an exhausting eighteen-hour flight, Master Sergeant Barbara J. Dulinsky arrived at Bien Hoa Air Force Base, thirty miles from Saigon. When she stepped off the plane, she became the first female marine to serve in a combat zone. She didn't wear combat fatigues or carry a gun: Dulinsky served as an administrative chief with the Military Assistance Command.

Dulinsky was born on October 18, 1928, in San Francisco, California, and enlisted in the marines in 1951. She had been the senior drill instructor for women at Marine Corps Recruit Depot Parris Island, South Carolina, before volunteering for service in Vietnam. Parris Island has been an active site of Marine Corps training since World War I.

"She volunteered [for the assignment in Vietnam] at a time she did not think she was going to get it," said Nancy Wilt, curator for the Women of the Corps Collection of the Women Marines Association. "It was pie in the sky.... I think she was shocked she got it."

Volunteering to serve in Vietnam may have opened up opportunities to career advancement. "Women were looking for career-enhancing moves and she saw she could do it, and she did it," said Wilt.

When she arrived in Saigon, Dulinsky had to go through extensive security briefings, learning how to recognize booby traps and dangers in an area that remained very dangerous. She served for one year—from 1967 to 1968—processing correspondence and maintaining more than 5,000 classified documents.

Dulinsky was one of only thirty-six female marines to serve in Vietnam between 1967 and 1973. She retired from the Marine Corps in 1974 and lived in San Francisco, California, then Kent, Washington. She died there of natural causes on March 28, 1995, at age sixty-six.

IN HER OWN WORDS

"The first question most generally asked about my tour in Vietnam, was it voluntary? Well, yes and no." Master Sergeant Barbara Dulinsky said. "In February 1967, I was completing a tour as First Sergeant of Recruit Company, Woman Recruit Training Battalion, Marine Corps Recruit Depot, Parris Island, South Carolina. As anyone who has served in a Recruit Training Command, when your tour is completed, you're ready to go, but not necessarily to Vietnam."

When a major from Marine Corps Headquarters called and asked Sergeant Dulinsky if she was interested in serving in Saigon, Vietnam, she said: "Major, you've got to be out of your mind. I'm a devout coward."

Dulinsky knew the risk of serving in Vietnam. At the time, the news media were reporting frequent terrorist attacks by the Viet Cong in Saigon.

"I just felt anyone volunteering for such duty had to be partially demented or lacked a full sea bag," she said.

She resisted a couple of additional phone calls from Headquarters, then she agreed to serve. Despite the risks involved with her assignment, when asked if she could do it over again, she said: "Would I ever do it again? I'm sure I would. Always a new challenge—something different."

This excerpt is from an unpublished memoir held in the Archives and Special Collections branch of the Library of the Marine Corps.

ALENE B. DUERK:
THE NAVY'S FIRST ADMIRAL

ALENE B. DUERK

Alene B. Duerk entered the Nurse Corps of the United States Naval Reserve in 1943 as a young nurse with limited experience. When she left the armed forces thirty-two years later, she retired as the director of the Navy Nurse Corps and the navy's first female admiral.

Alene Bertha Duerk was born on March 29, 1920, in Defiance, Ohio. When she was a child, her father was very ill, and nurses were in their house a lot. Alene saw this and it became her first dealings with nursing as a profession. Alene went to nursing school and graduated from the Toledo Hospital School of Nursing in 1941. She joined the Nurse Corps two years later, in 1943, to put her skills to use in service to her country. During her career, she worked at naval

Navy Rear Admiral Alene Duerk received the Distinguished Alumni Award from Case Western Reserve University's Frances Payne Bolton School of Nursing in 1974.

hospitals in Maryland, Virginia, Illinois, and Michigan. After serving during World War II, she went back to school for additional training in ward management and teaching from Case Western Reserve University in Cleveland, Ohio. She graduated in 1948. She then served in the Korean War and the Vietnam War.

She always taught her students teamwork and communication. "Each of us must not only be able to communicate our knowledge and understanding to the other team members, but also our needs and the needs of our departments or services," Duerk said. "In turn, each of us must listen as others talk with us. The listening side of communication is the most difficult."

For decades, women had limited opportunities for advancement in the navy. In 1972, when the United States adopted an all-volunteer forces policy, military leadership began to promote women and give them more responsibility. Duerk proved ready, willing, and able to serve, becoming the director of the Navy Nurse Corps in 1970 and the first female admiral in the navy in 1972. As director of the Navy Nurse Corps, Duerk pushed for promotional opportunities and pay increases for nurses.

She retired from the navy in 1975. On July 21, 2018, Alene B. Duerk died at the age of ninety-eight in her home in Lake Mary, Florida.

ANNA MAE HAYS AND ELIZABETH P. HOISINGTON: THE GENERALS

Anna Mae Hays and Elizabeth P. Hoisington

It took almost two hundred years for the United States Army to promote a woman to the rank of brigadier general. It took only minutes for the promotion of the second. On June 11, 1970, Anna Mae Hays, chief of the Army Nurse Corps, became the first female brigadier general, and a few minutes later, as part of the same ceremony, Elizabeth Hoisington, director of the Women's Army Corps, became the second.

Anna Mae Hays was born on February 16, 1920, in Buffalo, New York. Both her parents worked for the Salvation Army, and the family moved several times, finally settling in Allentown, Pennsylvania. After high school, Hays went to nursing school, graduating from Allentown General Hospital School of Nursing in 1941.

After the attack on Pearl Harbor, Hays wanted to enlist. "The war was declared on 7 December 1941, and from that time until I joined in May of 1942, the papers were full of stories about individuals serving their country," she told the Army Heritage Center Foundation in 1983. "Being a nurse, I too wanted to serve my country."

When World War II began, Hays joined the Army Nurse Corps and deployed to the Twentieth General Hospital in India. The conditions there were challenging: she lived and worked in bamboo huts, and she had to deal with leeches, snakes, and diseases, such as dysentery, spread through unsafe drinking water.

After the war, Hays remained on active duty. During the Korean War, she mobilized with the Fourth Field Hospital, which cared for an astonishing 25,000 patients between September 1950 and July 1951. One night the hospital received an overwhelming 700 patients, and she and the other nurses had to care for them with insufficient supplies in the bitter cold.

"If you would ask me what are the first things you can remember about Korea, I would say its cold weather, odor, and its stark-nakedness," she told the Army Heritage Center. "And, when I compare Korea with my experiences in World War II, I think of Korea as even worse than the jungle in World War II, because of the lack of supplies, lack of warmth, etc., in the operating room."

In 1954, Hays became head nurse for the emergency room at the army's flagship hospital, Walter Reed Army Medical Center in Washington, DC. When President Dwight Eisenhower was hospitalized there, she was one of three nurses responsible for his care.

Hays climbed in rank throughout her career, becoming chief of the Army Nurse Corps and a full colonel in 1967. During the Vietnam War, she reviewed the conditions under which her nurses were deployed. Hays retired on August 31, 1971, before the end of the war.

In 1970, women finally broke through the "brass ceiling" and became generals in the army. Hays won the distinction of becoming the first brigadier general because when listed alphabetically her name came before that of Elizabeth P. Hoisington, technically the second woman to become a brigadier general.

Elizabeth Paschel Hoisington was born in Newton, Kansas, on November 3, 1918. Her father had been a colonel in the army and a noted marksman. When Elizabeth was a young girl, her father taught her how to ride horses and to handle a gun. In 1940, she graduated from the College of Notre Dame of Maryland, and in 1942 she enlisted in the Women's Army Auxiliary Corps.

"The minute she heard about the WAC, she wanted to join," said Elizabeth's sister, Nancy

Smith. "She went in as a private and came out as a general."

Hoisington completed basic training and then applied to Officer Candidate School. Before starting the program, she found a tough and experienced sergeant and asked him for tips on surviving officer training. She often said that he did such a good job briefing her that she breezed through the program.

She was commissioned a second lieutenant in the Women's Army Corps and deployed to France just after D-Day during World War II. During her career, she steadily climbed in rank as she served in Japan, Germany, France, and the Pentagon. She became director of the Women's Army Corps in 1965 and was promoted to brigadier general in 1970. "We were always just as much officers as any other officer," she said in 1988. "To those who say we weren't, hell to them. I wasn't in the Salvation Army. The WAC was just like any other corps."

In addition to being recognized as the second female general, Hoisington and her brother, Perry M. Hoisington II, have the distinction of being the first brother and sister generals in American history; Perry M. Hoisington II was a major general in the United States Air Force.

Hoisington retired on August 1, 1971, a month before Hays. She died of congestive heart failure in Springfield, Virginia, in 2007 at age eighty-eight. Hays died from a heart attack at age ninety-seven in 2018.

Hays married in 1956 and was widowed in 1962. Hoisington never married. When asked about her personal life in 1970, Hoisington said: "The Army is my first love."

THE "BRASS CEILING"

The "glass ceiling" is an expression used to describe an invisible barrier that keeps women and minorities from top-level positions in business and government. The term "brass ceiling" refers to the same problem in the military and law enforcement, where "brass" is a term for high-ranking officers with lots of medals. Breaking the brass ceiling means women and minorities are finally being promoted to the highest positions.

REVEREND ALICE M. HENDERSON:
THE FIRST FEMALE CHAPLAIN

ALICE M. HENDERSON

In 1863, the United States Army commissioned its first African American chaplain. It took another 111 years to allow a woman—who also happened to be African American—to serve as an army chaplain. In 1974, Reverend Alice M. Henderson, a minister in the African Methodist Episcopal Church, became the first female army chaplain. She served with the 426th Signal Battalion at Fort Bragg, North Carolina. She was one of 1,467 chaplains in the army at the time.

Henderson was born in Indian Springs, Georgia, in 1947. Growing up, she wanted a career as a pop singer. She changed her mind during her studies at Clark College (now Clark-Atlanta University); instead of studying music, she graduated in 1968 with a degree in

Rev. Alice M. Henderson served as the first female chaplain in the army. She was commissioned in 1974 and retired from the military after thirteen years of service.

religion and philosophy. She then attended Turner Theological Center of the Interdenominational Theological Center in Atlanta. Although she grew up Baptist, she changed to the African Methodist Episcopal Church because she thought it would have more opportunities for women in ministry.

She was ordained in 1969 and served as an associate minister at the Cobb Bethel AME Church in Atlanta. She didn't get a church assignment after graduation from seminary, so she decided to apply for a chaplain's job with the army. "I was more surprised than anyone when I found out that they had no women chaplains," she said. She attended Army Chaplain School in Fort Hamilton, New York, in 1974. She was then sent to Fort Bragg.

During her thirteen years of service as a member of the Chaplain Corps of the army, Henderson held religious services and offered counseling and moral support to members of her military unit. Rev. Henderson became a trusted counselor and support to the women and men in her battalion.

THE CHAPLAIN CORPS

Chaplains have been part of the military since 1775, providing religious support to soldiers. Soldiers can practice any religion—or no religion at all. The military is supported by the Army Chaplain Corps, the Air Force Chaplain Corps, and the Navy Chaplain Corps, which also serves the Marine Corps, the merchant marines, and the coast guard.

The corps is made up of clergy from different religious backgrounds, including Buddhism, Catholicism, Eastern Orthodox Christianity, Islam, Judaism, and Protestantism. Chaplains have noncombatant status and they do not carry weapons.

While the Chaplain Corps has always attempted to be open to people of a variety of faiths, the military has been slow to admit women of non-Christian faiths to the Chaplain Corps. Chaplain Colonel Bonnie Koppell became the first female rabbi officially endorsed as a military chaplain in 1981. Chaplain Captain Pratima Dharm became the army's first Hindu chaplain in 2011.

JEANNE M. HOLM:
SEEING STARS

JEANNE M. HOLM

D uring her career in the military, Jeanne M. Holm didn't just become the highest-ranking woman serving in the United States Air Force, she became the highest-ranking woman serving in *all* branches of the armed forces.

Holm was born on June 23, 1921, in Portland, Oregon. Like many women in the armed forces at the time, she enlisted in the Women's Army Auxiliary Corps in 1942 so that she could support her country during World War II. She attended Officer Candidate School and was commissioned as a third officer, a rank equal to second lieutenant in the male army. She commanded a basic training company and then she oversaw an entire regiment.

After the war, Holm commanded the 106th Women's Army Corps Hospital Company in

Air force major general Jeanne M. Holm was the first woman in the military to become a two-star general. Holm wrote two books, *Women in the Military: An Unfinished Revolution* (1982) and *In Defense of a Nation: Servicewomen in World War II* (1998).

WELCOME BACK

Enlisting in the military involves signing a contract that obligates the recruit to a particular term of service, typically eight years. After a period of active duty, usually three or four years, a soldier returns to civilian life but is assigned to the Individual Ready Reserve (IRR) for the balance of their contract. While on IRR, military personnel can be recalled for service in response to a national emergency.

Military personnel who serve twenty years and retire can be recalled at any time, but recall is highly unlikely after five years of retirement or after age sixty.

West Virginia. She left the military to earn her college degree from Lewis and Clark College, but was recalled in 1948 to serve as a company commander within the Women's Army Corps Training Center.

When the air force opened to women, Holm transferred and served in a number of jobs, helping organize the early efforts of the Korean War. In 1952, she became the first woman to attend the Air Command and Staff College at Maxwell Air Force Base in Montgomery, Alabama, and was assigned to the air force headquarters in Washington, DC.

In 1965, Holm became the director of Women in the Air Force, responsible for advising on issues involving women in the air force. She was able to double the number of women serving and expand the number of job assignments available to females.

In addition, Holm opened the Reserve Officers' Training Corps to college women, and she paved the way for women to attend the Air Force Academy in Colorado Springs. She also facilitated making the air force the first branch of the armed service in which a woman commanded a mixed unit of men and women.

On July 16, 1971, Holm became the first woman promoted to the grade of brigadier general in the air force. Two years later, she was promoted again, becoming the first major general in any branch of the armed services. She retired from the air force in 1975.

In 2003, the Air Force Association conferred upon Holm their Lifetime Achievement Award. She was inducted into the International Women in Aviation Hall of Fame in 2006. On February 15, 2010, she died from pneumonia in Annapolis, Maryland, at age eighty-eight.

SHARON ANN LANE:
PAYING THE ULTIMATE PRICE

Days before the attack, army nurse First Lieutenant Sharon Ann Lane wrote home, telling her family that things in Chu Lai, Vietnam, had been unusually quiet. When the hospital where she was working came under fire days later, she earned the unfortunate distinction of becoming the first—and only—military woman killed by enemy fire during the Vietnam War.

Sharon Ann Lane was born July 7, 1943, in Zanesville, Ohio. She spent most of her childhood in Canton, graduating from Canton South High School in 1961. She went on to the Aultman Hospital School of Nursing, graduating in 1965, and then worked at a local hospital. In 1968, she joined the United States Army Nurse Corps Reserve, training in Texas and then working at the army's Fitzsimons General Hospital in Denver, Colorado. In 1969 she was ordered to Vietnam.

On April 29, 1969, Lane was assigned to the intensive care unit of the 312th Evacuation Hospital at Chu Lai. Less than six weeks later, on June 8, 1969, the hospital was hit by rocket fire, and Lane was one of two people killed. She was twenty-five years old. She was awarded the Purple Heart, the Bronze Star Medal, the National Defense Service Medal, among other honors.

SHARON ANN LANE

BARBARA ANN ALLEN RAINEY:

EARNING HER WINGS

BARBARA ANN ALLEN RAINEY

Women had been flying planes for decades, but Lieutenant Junior Grade Barbara Ann Allen Rainey became the first woman in the United States Navy to earn her wings as a naval aviator on February 22, 1974. She also became the first navy woman to qualify as a jet pilot.

Barbara Ann Allen was born on August 20, 1948, in Bethesda, Maryland. She grew up with a respect for the military since both of her parents were navy officers. After attending Long Beach City College in California, Barbara joined the Navy Reserve in 1970.

When she learned that the navy was creating a test program to train female pilots in 1973, Barbara applied to the Naval Flight Training School. She was one of eight women chosen for the program, and she became the first to complete training. During training school, she met Lieutenant Commander John C. Rainey, and they later married.

Barbara excelled at both flying and teaching others to fly. In 1981, she became a flight instructor. Tragically, on July 13, 1982, Barbara Allen Rainey, as well as the trainee, Ensign Donald Bruce Knowlton, died in a plane crash at Middleton Field near Evergreen, Alabama. She was thirty-three years old.

DO YOU HAVE WHAT IT TAKES
TO BE A NAVAL AVIATOR?

Soldiers must meet a series of qualifications to be considered for training to become a naval pilot:

- Age 19 to 27
- An undergraduate degree with a minimum grade point average of 2.0
- 20/40 vision correctable to 20/20
- Color vision
- Normal depth perception
- Height: 62"–78" (male); 58"–78" (female)
- Able to swim
- Weight under 235 pounds

Candidates who complete training are obligated to serve a minimum of eight years in active duty.

Student pilots learn basic airmanship, instrument and formation flying, and basic acrobatic maneuvers. Intermediate training is specialized, and soldiers are divided into one of five "pipelines:" jet, turboprop, multi-engine jet, carrier turboprop, and helicopter.

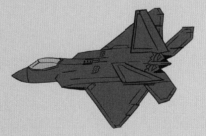

APPROACHING EQUALITY:

WOMEN IN THE MODERN MILITARY

Gone are the days when women needed to pretend to be men to enlist in the military. Gone are the days when women could serve only as nurses and cooks and laundry workers. Gone are the days of women being used in support roles only when the military needed extra hands during wartime. There is no going backward: after the Vietnam War, changes in American culture—particularly the achievements of the women's movement—solidified the role of women in the military. It was clear that women had a lot to offer to the armed forces and that their services were needed.

One of the initial and most important signs of meaningful change came in 1976 when the first females were admitted to the service academies: the Military Academy at West Point, New York; the Naval Academy at Annapolis, Maryland; the Coast Guard Academy in New London, Connecticut; and the Air Force Academy in Colorado Springs, Colorado. In the first year the doors were opened, more than 350 women entered these programs.

The courts also forced the military to provide more opportunities for women. Historically women had not been allowed to serve on navy and marine ships. Yona Owens, a woman who worked as a navy electrician, filed a class action suit arguing that women should have the right to serve on military ships. In the 1978 case *Owens v. Brown*, the United States Supreme Court determined that she was right, and women gained the right to serve on noncombat ships as technicians, nurses, and officers.

This legal change extended beyond the navy. All branches of the armed services opened more positions to females and gave women a chance to compete for leadership roles. This change brought a generation of firsts for women, as females took on new responsibilities and rose through the ranks. Women of color also broke barriers, proving that women of all racial backgrounds could be exemplary leaders if given the chance.

Over the next twenty years, ideas about women in the military changed as the nature of warfare changed. New weapons—such as short-range mobile missiles and roadside bombs—redefined the front lines of war, leaving every soldier at risk of injury or death. Women didn't take on combat roles, but combat came to them.

Despite the increased risk, women continued to enlist and serve in the military.

When the Iraqi army invaded Kuwait in 1990, the United States and thirty-five other nations responded by sending troops into the area. For the first time, American men and women shipped out together in wartime conditions. When the USS *Acadia* left for the Persian Gulf on September 5, 1990, almost one-third of the soldiers on board were women. When the war ended in 1991, more than 40,000 women had served in the Gulf War.

Women served honorably in that conflict, but the nation had not yet made peace with the idea of women actively fighting in war. The military wanted to be able to use women in aviation units, so it issued a new rule that opened additional opportunities to female soldiers. In 1994 the Department of Defense implemented the combat exclusion policy, stating that women could be assigned to all positions for which they are qualified, except ground combat.

Women played critical roles in the wars in Iraq and Afghanistan. By 2009, the military had established female engagement teams, all-female Marine Corps teams that went into various communities and distributed information and gathered intelligence from women in Afghanistan.

The combat exclusion policy had an impact on women's careers because high-level promotions often required combat experience. If women could not serve in combat, they could not qualify for the top leadership positions. The final frontier in discrimination was the battlefield.

Finally, in 2013, the Defense Department announced that the military would allow women to serve in all military roles within the next three years.

"If members of our military can meet the qualifications for a job, then they should have the right to serve, regardless of creed, color, gender, or sexual orientation," said Defense Secretary Leon E. Panetta.

The policy was fully implemented in January 2016: all jobs were opened to women. "They'll be allowed to drive tanks, fire mortars, and lead infantry soldiers into combat," said Defense Secretary Ash Carter. "They'll be able to serve as Army Rangers and Green Berets, Navy SEALs, Marine Corps infantry, Air Force parajumpers, and everything else that was previously open only to men."

Today, women make up about 15 percent

of the U.S. military. More than 200,000 women are enlisted in the armed services and more than 35,000 others serve as officers. In 2017, the first 18 women graduated from the army's first gender-integrated infantry basic training. As long as they meet the requirements for the job, women can serve in any position in any branch of the military.

RECENT CONFLICTS

The **Gulf War** (1990–1991) was fought between Iraq and a coalition of thirty-five countries, led by the United States. It is also known as the Persian Gulf War, First Gulf War, and by the code names Operation Desert Shield (August 2, 1990–January 17, 1991) and Operation Desert Storm (January 17, 1991–February 28, 1991). It was fought in response to Iraq's invasion of Kuwait.

The **Iraq War** (2003–2011) began with the overthrow of the government of Saddam Hussein and the invasion of Iraq by the United States and coalition forces. It is also known as the Second Persian Gulf War and Operation Desert Freedom.

The **Afghanistan War** (2001–present) began following the 2001 invasion of Afghanistan by the United States, an action that was later supported by a coalition of more than forty countries. The objective is to remove the Taliban from power and end the operations of the terrorist group al-Qaeda.

The **Iraqi Civil War** (2014–present) is an armed conflict between the Iraqi government and Islamic State of Iraq and Syria (ISIS). The United States has carried out air strikes and offered support to the Iraqi government.

GWENDOLYN BINGHAM:
"THE HEART OF A LION"

GWENDOLYN BINGHAM

Lieutenant General Gwendolyn McMillion Bingham grew up knowing that she wanted to be part of the military. "Quite honestly, I think I was hooked from the moment I walked on a parade field with my dad," she said.

Born in 1959, Gwendolyn McMillion grew up in Troy, Alabama, and studied business management at the University of Alabama on an ROTC (Reserve Officers' Training Corps) scholarship. At first, she thought she would serve four years in the military and then get a civilian job after being discharged, but her plans changed.

When Gwendolyn graduated from college in 1981, her father, twenty-year army veteran First Sergeant Edward McMillion, pinned her second lieutenant bars on her uniform during the ceremony in which she was commissioned in the Quartermaster Corps. During her career, Gwendolyn worked her way up the ranks of the Quartermaster Corps, the branch of the military responsible for distributing fuel, food, water, and other supplies to troops around the world. (The Quartermaster Corps furnishes everything except ammunition and medical supplies. It even handles the retrieval, transportation, and burial of those who die during their service.) She also married Dr. Patrick J. Bingham, and they have two children.

Lieutenant General Bingham became used to being first: she was the first female garrison commander at Fort Lee, Virginia; the first female commandant of the U.S. Army Quartermaster School at Fort Lee; the first female quartermaster general; and the first female commanding general of the White Sands Missile Range, New Mexico. She served in operations Iraqi Freedom and Enduring Freedom. She became a three-star general.

She was known to fight for what she believed in. At the promotion ceremony when she became a brigadier general, Major General James E. Chambers said, "Inside, she has the heart of a lion." Bingham is the current assistant chief of staff for Installation Management, advising the chief of staff about facility management, morale, welfare, recreation, and family support programs.

COLONEL EILEEN COLLINS:
"THE GREATEST ADVENTURE ON THIS PLANET—OR OFF"

During her career, Colonel Eileen Collins logged 38 days, 8 hours, and 20 minutes in outer space. She also became the first female to serve as a space shuttle commander. While her exploration of space wasn't a part of her military service, Colonel Collins began her career in flight with the United States Air Force.

Eileen Marie Collins was born on November 19, 1956, in Elmira, New York. Her fascination with flight began when she was in fourth grade. "I remember sitting at my desk, reading an article in *Junior Scholastic* magazine on the Gemini astronauts. Although there were no women astronauts in the article, that did not seem to bother me. I just thought, 'I will be a woman astronaut!'"

She wanted to take flying lessons, but her family couldn't afford it. So during high school Collins worked nights at a pizza parlor, saving money to go to flight school. When she was nineteen, she climbed aboard a plane for the first time. Immediately, she knew she wanted to be a pilot.

But first, Collins needed an education. After graduating from Elmira Free Academy in 1974, she earned an associate degree in mathematics and science from Corning Community College and a bachelor's degree in mathematics and economics from Syracuse University in 1978. She went on to earn two master's degrees—one in 1986 in operations research from Stanford University and one in 1989 in space systems management from Webster University.

Following graduation from Syracuse, she was one of only four women chosen for undergraduate pilot training at Vance Air Force Base, Oklahoma. After earning her pilot wings, she stayed on as a flight instructor for several years. She became an assistant professor of mathematics at the Air Force Academy in Colorado, as well as a flight instructor.

In 1989, she became the second female pilot to attend the United States Air Force Test Pilot School, and the following year NASA (National Aeronautics and Space Administration) chose her for the astronaut program. While NASA and the air force have different missions, they have a close relationship and often share launch facilities, exchange information, and work toward common goals.

Collins made it to space as pilot of the space shuttle *Discovery* in 1995 and again on board the space shuttle *Atlantis* in 1997. She became the first female space shuttle commander on the 1999 *Columbia* mission. In 2003, seven crew members were killed and the *Columbia* was destroyed in a tragic explosion. Two years later, Collins commanded the *Discovery* on a mission to resupply the International Space Station.

In 2005, Collins retired from the air force and in 2006 from NASA. "I wanted to be part of our nation's space program," she said. "It's the greatest adventure on this planet—or off the planet, for that matter." During her career, Colonel Eileen Collins received the Distinguished Flying Cross, Defense Meritorious Service Medal, Air Force Meritorious Service Medal, French Legion of Honor, and NASA Outstanding Leadership Medal, among other honors.

SARAH DEAL:
A PILOT AND A MARINE

SARAH DEAL

Sarah Deal wanted to be a pilot—but she also wanted to be a United States Marine. At first, she assumed she would have to make a choice because she didn't think she could do both. At the time Deal was thinking about enlisting—in 1992—the marines did not allow women in the cockpit, even though the navy and air force had been welcoming women aviators for decades.

Growing up, Deal knew she wanted to follow her father into the Marine Corps. She was born in Bowling Green, Ohio, on September 14, 1969. When she was a child, her family moved to a small town outside Toledo, Ohio, where Deal worked on a dairy farm, ran track, and played baseball. She was active in 4-H, and every year she raised a pig that she would

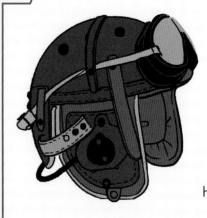

sell at auction. Her school celebrated its rural roots with an annual drive-your-tractor-to-school day. Deal loved rural life, but she wanted something her small town didn't offer: she wanted to fly.

Deal studied aerospace flight technology at Kent State University, graduating in 1992. She earned her pilot's license in college and participated in a precision flight team, but she assumed she was going to have to set aside her ambition as a pilot in order to join the Marine Corps.

In 1992, Deal was commissioned as a second lieutenant. She completed basic training and requested an assignment in aviation maintenance; she wanted to be near airplanes, even if she couldn't fly them. When the Marine Corps changed its policy the following year, she was allowed to transfer to flight training school at the Naval Air Station Pensacola, Florida. She specialized as a helicopter pilot, and in 1995 she became the first female marine to earn her aviator's wings.

In 2004, she transferred to the Marine Corps Reserve. In 2009, she deployed to Afghanistan during Operation Enduring Freedom. During her service she often flew ten- to eleven-hour missions in heat so extreme that the pilots had to wear gloves in order to touch the instruments without burning their hands! Despite the challenges, Deal was delighted: she was able to serve her country in the way she had imagined, as a Marine Corps pilot.

TAMMY DUCKWORTH:
A SOLDIER AND A SENATOR

On November 12, 2004, Lieutenant Colonel Tammy Duckworth was copiloting a Black Hawk helicopter in Iraq when a rocket-propelled grenade exploded directly underneath the cockpit of her aircraft. Duckworth survived the attack, but she lost both her legs—her right leg near the hip and her left leg below the knee—as well as the use of her right arm.

Duckworth became the first female double amputee from the Iraq War. But her injuries didn't stop her from wanting to serve. She requested and received a medical waiver from the army and continued to serve in the Illinois Army National Guard for ten more years.

TAMMY DUCKWORTH

Duckworth's family had a long history of military service. Her father, a marine who served in World War II, could trace his family tree back to soldiers who fought in the Revolutionary War. Duckworth's mother was from Thailand, and her parents met when her father worked with the United Nations and international companies in Southeast Asia. Duckworth was born in Bangkok, Thailand, on March 12, 1968, and she attended schools in Singapore and Bangkok. She came to the United States for college and graduated from the University of Hawaii in 1989 with a degree in political science.

As a graduate student in international affairs at George Washington University,

Duckworth decided to follow in the footsteps of her father and other family members who had served in the military. She joined the Army Reserve Officers' Training Corps, and in 1992, she became a commissioned officer. She chose to fly helicopters, one of the only combat jobs available to women.

In 2004, Duckworth was deployed to Iraq. Her helicopter was shot down several months later. She received the Purple Heart and Army Commendation Medal, and thirteen months after the attack, she was standing on titanium legs and trying to learn how to fly again.

After the accident, Duckworth worked on behalf of other veterans. She served as director of the Illinois Department of Veterans Affairs and then as assistant secretary for Public and Intergovernmental Affairs for the Department of Veterans Affairs. She retired from the army in 2014.

She decided she could best serve the public and advocate for veterans' issues by running for public office. She became the first Asian American female soldier elected to Congress in Illinois in 2012. She was also the first disabled woman elected to Congress and the first member of Congress to have been born in Thailand. After serving two terms as a Democrat in the United States House of Representatives, she was elected senator from Illinois in 2016. In 2018, she broke another barrier when she got the Senate to change its rules so that she could bring her newborn daughter onto the floor of the Senate when she had to cast a vote.

Duckworth has always strived to maintain a positive attitude. In a 2016 interview with GQ magazine she commented on her injuries: "You can choose to cry about it, and you can choose to be depressed for the rest of your life about it, but at the end of the day, I earned my injuries. I earned this. And I'm proud that I earned this. Because I earned it in defense of my nation." Every November 12, Duckworth and her three Black Hawk crewmates celebrate what they call "Alive Day," a recognition of the anniversary of the accident that they survived in Iraq in 2004.

ANN ELIZABETH DUNWOODY:
ANSWERING THE CALL

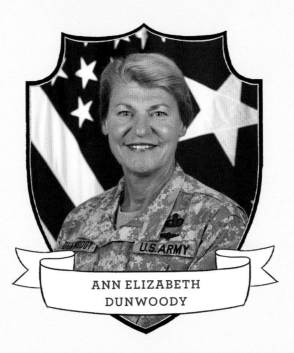

ANN ELIZABETH
DUNWOODY

A nn Elizabeth Dunwoody had an impeccable military pedigree. Her great-grandfather graduated from West Point. So did her grandfather and her father, Brigadier General Harold Dunwoody, who earned two Purple Hearts and a Distinguished Service Cross for valor during service in World War II, the Korean War, and the Vietnam War.

But Ann Dunwoody didn't want to serve in the military. From the age of five, she was certain that she wanted to be a physical education teacher and coach. She was born on January 14, 1953, at Fort Belvoir, Virginia, but she grew up in Germany and Belgium, where her father was serving in the army.

After high school, Dunwoody returned to the United States and enrolled at the State

During her career, Ann Elizabeth Dunwoody received the Army Distinguished
Service Medal and the Defense Superior Service Medal, among many other honors.

University of New York College at Cortland to study physical education. But things began to change during her junior year of college. Dunwoody attended a four-week army introductory program so that she could better understand the call to military service that had been such an important part of her family's legacy. She followed that with an eleven-week Women's Officer Orientation Course. By then, the urge to serve was great, and in 1975, she enlisted in the army's Quartermaster Corps as a second lieutenant. At that point, Dunwoody still thought she would complete her two-year commitment and then become a physical education teacher, but once she was part of the military she couldn't imagine doing anything else.

Dunwoody spent thirty-seven years rising through the ranks in the army. In 2005, she became the army's top-ranking woman when she was promoted to lieutenant general—a three-star general—and she took over as the army's deputy chief of staff, logistics. In 2008, she was promoted to four-star general, the first female four-star general and the highest-ranking woman in the history of the armed services.

In the military, she never served under a female superior. "I've always had male bosses who have coached me, mentored me, and influenced my career as a soldier," Dunwoody said. "[They are] leaders who opened the doors for me, leaders who looked beyond gender, leaders who could see something in folks that didn't look like they do."

During her career, Dunwoody managed the largest logistics division in the history of the army—a $60 billion operation that included nearly 70,000 people, located in 50 states and more than 140 countries. She retired from the army on August 15, 2012. "Over the last thirty-eight years I have had the opportunity to witness women soldiers jump out of airplanes, hike ten miles, lead men and women, even under the toughest circumstances," Dunwoody said. "And today, women are in combat, that is just a reality. Thousands of women have been decorated for valor and 146 have given their lives. Today, what was once a band of brothers has truly become a band of brothers and sisters."

SHERRI GALLAGHER:
SOLDIER OF THE YEAR

Sherri Jo Gallagher fired a rifle for the first time when she was five years old. Before she turned twenty, she was the World Long Range Shooting Champion, and the National Rifle Association had named her National Rifle Champion—twice.

Gallagher was born in California in 1984 and grew up in Prescott, Arizona. She enlisted in the army in 2008. "It was something that I felt I should do for my country," she said. Gallagher became an instructor on the Army Marksmanship Unit and continued to compete. In 2010, she became the second woman to win the National High Power Rifle Championship; the first woman in history to win the honor had been her mother.

SHERRI GALLAGHER

In 2010, Gallagher competed for Soldier of the Year, a contest for the best-all-around soldier, based on hand-to-hand combat, urban orienteering, and night firing, among other skills. Gallagher won the 2010 title, becoming the first woman to win the award.

She excelled in the rifle qualification. "It was faster-paced, quick, reactive shooting, but all shooting's the same," Gallagher said. "Keep your sights aligned and you're good. I'm always more comfortable with a gun in my hand."

Staff Sergeant Sherri Gallagher holds twenty-two national rifle records. In addition to marksmanship, Gallagher is an expert skydiver. She was invited to join the army's Golden Knights Parachute Team in 2012.

CAPTAIN KRISTEN GRIEST AND LIEUTENANT SHAYE HAVER: LEADING THE WAY

Captain Kristen Marie Griest

It's tough to become an Army Ranger, the elite group of brave and superfit soldiers who often deploy on the riskiest missions. Only about 3 percent of all soldiers serving in the army qualify as Rangers. The group's motto is "Rangers lead the way." Leading the way for women in the military are two soldiers—Captain Kristen Griest and Lieutenant Shaye Haver—who in 2015 became the **FIRST** women to graduate from Ranger School at Fort Benning, Georgia. The sixty-one-day course is considered one of the premier military leadership programs in the world.

Their graduation marked an important change in military culture: from that moment on, no one could question the grit and determination of women serving in the military. Secretary of the Army John M. McHugh said at the time of the graduation, "This course has proven that every soldier, regardless of gender, can achieve his or her full potential."

Before going through Ranger School, Griest graduated from the United States Military Academy at West Point in 2011 and served in Afghanistan as a military police officer. Haver graduated from West Point the following year and served as an Apache attack helicopter pilot. Both women were eager to prove themselves by enrolling in Ranger School in the spring of 2015, when the army launched a one-time pilot program to see if women could qualify for the highly competitive outfit.

In April 2015, 400 soldiers—380 men and 20 women—entered Ranger School. During the combat leadership training, soldiers learn to overcome stress,

Lieutenant Shaye Lynne Haver

hunger, and fatigue and to lead small-unit operations. On average, 60 percent of those who qualify to enter Ranger School don't make it to graduation because it is so grueling.

Like many other soldiers, Griest and Haver failed the first phase of the training, in which students must pass tests of stamina, mental toughness, and leadership. But instead of dropping out, Griest and Haver were given the chance to do a Day 1 recycle and start over. They were not the only ones to do so; many men don't make it through the first time either.

During the program, there were times when Griest and Haver wanted to quit, but they refused to give up. "I was thinking really of future generations of women . . . ," Griest said, "so I had that pressure on myself."

Critics claimed that the performance standards were lowered for women, but that was not the case. Major General Scott Miller, the commanding general of the Army Maneuver Center of Excellence at Fort Benning, said there was no change to the standards. "There was no pressure from anyone above me to change standards," he said. "Standards remain the same."

Griest and Haver graduated along with ninety-four men in August 2015. A third female soldier, Major Lisa Jester (also a West Point graduate), completed the course a few months later, in October 2015.

Even after graduating from Ranger School, the women were not allowed to serve in the unit because it was part of the infantry—the fighting forces. At the time the military still excluded women from combat positions. But that changed in late 2015, and in 2016 Kristen Griest became the first female infantry officer in the army. She was assigned to the 4th Ranger Training Battalion of the Airborne and Ranger Training Brigade at Fort Benning, Georgia.

Haver enjoyed her work as a helicopter pilot. Rather than switch to the infantry, she chose to remain an attack helicopter pilot—one who proudly wore the black-and-gold Ranger tab on her uniform.

MARCELITE J. HARRIS:
BREAKING BARRIERS

MARCELITE J. HARRIS

Throughout American history, it has been difficult for women to enter the military and get the respect they deserve, and that challenge has been still greater for women of color. Despite the obstacles, Marcelite Harris was able to rise through the ranks and become the first African American female air force one-star general in 1991 and the first two-star general in 1995.

Marcelite Jordan Harris was born on January 16, 1943, in Houston, Texas. She graduated from Spelman College with a degree in speech and drama in 1964 before joining the Women in the Air Force program. The Vietnam War was raging, but she wanted to enlist so that she could travel the world while serving her country. She went through Officer Training School

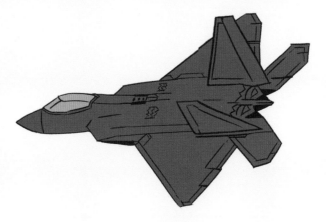

at Lackland Air Force Base in Texas and specialized in aircraft maintenance. During the Vietnam War she served at an air base in Thailand and later at the Air Force Academy in Colorado.

Her career included many firsts: she was the first female aircraft maintenance officer, one of the first two female commanders at the Air Force Academy, and the first female air force director of maintenance. While serving as director of maintenance, Harris managed a workforce of more than 125,000 people and maintained the more than $260 billion aerospace weapons system inventory. She became the first African American female brigadier general of the air force in 1990 and the first African American female major general in 1995.

In 1997, Harris retired as a major general, the highest-ranking female officer in the air force and the highest-ranking African American woman in any branch of the armed services. She received a number of major awards during her career, including the Legion of Merit, Bronze Star Medal, Meritorious Service Medal, Air Force Commendation Medal, Presidential Unit Citation, Air Force Outstanding Unit Award, Vietnamese Service Medal, and National Defense Service Medal, among others. After leaving the military, she served NASA as the Florida site director for United Space Alliance, the company that helped manage the space shuttle program. She also worked with the Atlanta Branch of the NAACP, the Board of Visitors for the Air Force Academy, and other organizations.

LEIGH ANN HESTER:

"I WAS TRAINED TO DO WHAT I DID"

LEIGH ANN HESTER

As a member of the 617th Military Police Company, Sergeant Leigh Ann Hester was used to having snipers occasionally fire a couple of rounds in her direction as she escorted military trucks along the supply routes in Iraq. But she wasn't prepared for what happened on the morning of March 20, 2005: it was an ambush.

At about 9 a.m. Hester and a squad of military police—eight men and two women—were following a thirty-truck supply convoy traveling near Salman Pak, Iraq. Suddenly a group of about fifty insurgent fighters attacked the convoy with machine gun fire and rocket-propelled grenades. Three members of her team were wounded.

Hester moved the truck to the side of the road, blocking the enemy's escape route. She and Staff Sergeant Timothy F. Nein attacked the fighters while hiding in a trench along the side of the road. The firefight and chaos lasted for nearly half an hour. When the battle was over, they had killed twenty-seven enemy fighters, wounded six, and captured one.

In recognition for her bravery, during a military awards ceremony at Camp Liberty, Iraq, Sergeant Hester was awarded the Silver Star on June 16, 2005. She is the first woman in United States history to earn the star medal for valor in combat.

Hester is modest about her achievement. "It's just something that happened one day," she said in an interview with NPR in 2011. "I was trained to do what I did, and I did it."

In addition to the Silver Star, Hester has received the Army Commendation Medal, National Defense Service Medal, Afghanistan Campaign Medal, Iraq Campaign Medal, and Armed Forces Reserve Medal, among other honors.

Leigh Ann Hester was born on January 12, 1982, in Bowling Green, Kentucky, and later moved to Nashville. She enlisted in the Army National Guard in the spring of 2001—before the 9/11 attacks—because she wanted to serve in the military police.

MARINA A. HIERL:
FIRST WOMAN TO LEAD AN INFANTRY PLATOON

The marines of Echo Company knew they were going to be assigned a new lieutenant, but when they finally met their new leader, they were shocked. Their new leader was a woman!

In 2018, twenty-four-year-old First Lieutenant Marina A. Hierl became the first woman in the Marine Corps to lead an infantry platoon when she took over as leader of the 2nd Battalion, 4th Marines' Echo Company.

Hierl grew up in Bethlehem, Pennsylvania. As a child, she didn't allow other people's expectations to define her. She joined her brother on his Boy Scout trips because she thought they were more exciting than Girl Scout outings. She also tried out for the high school wrestling team because there wasn't a girls' team.

Marina Hierl decided to enlist in the marines after graduating from the University of Southern California. "I wanted to do something important with my life," Hierl said. "I wanted to be part of a group of people that would be willing to die for each other." She graduated from the Marine Corps' Infantry Officer Course at Quantico, Virginia, in 2017.

At first, the men in her platoon second-guessed her ability to lead. But those suspicions were put to rest after she proved herself during a group exercise in the Mojave Desert.

Marina Hierl doesn't want to be known as the first female platoon leader. Instead, she wants to earn her reputation as a great platoon leader, period.

KATIE HIGGINS:
ANGELS IN THE SKY

KATIE HIGGINS

I n 1997, ten-year-old Katie Higgins attended an air show in California with her father, retired navy captain William Johnson. She watched with awe as the Blue Angels—the navy and Marine Corps flight demonstration squadron—flew in formation across the sky overhead. Twenty years later, Marine Corps captain Katie Higgins was invited to join the elite flight demonstration squadron, becoming the first female pilot to perform with the Blue Angels.

Higgins was attracted to the Blue Angels' mission of trying to recruit the next generation of pilots. "I loved the idea of going out and inspiring excellence to the American people," she said. "Not everybody needs to join the military but if everyone tries their hardest and does

their best at the profession that they choose, then it's better for the country and our society in general."

Higgins, a 2008 graduate of the Naval Academy, is a third-generation military pilot. She grew up on naval bases around the world. Her father flew the same Hornet jets that the Blue Angels do today. Two uncles and her grandfathers also served as pilots.

In July 2014, Higgins joined the six-member performance squad. During air shows, she flies the team's KC-130 Hercules support aircraft named Fat Albert in an eight-and-a-half-minute solo. Her showstopping routine includes a flyover at fifty feet, nosedives, and a touchdown that features a wheelie. When flying in formation, the Blue Angels fly as close as eighteen inches from wingtip to wingtip while performing a maneuver known as the Diamond 360.

"I definitely appreciate the support from the American people," Higgins said. "And if I can bring attention to opportunities people have in life, girls included—that they can join the military, be a Marine, even be a Blue Angel pilot, then that's cool."

While Higgins enjoys inspiring future pilots, she said that her most rewarding experience as a pilot did not occur on the show circuit. During a mission in Afghanistan in 2013, Higgins and her flight crew released a number of missiles that helped in the escape of a group of marines pinned down under enemy fire. She knew that her actions helped to save the lives of those marines in battle.

In a later mission, one of the marines who had been saved by Higgins recognized her voice on the radio. "He thanked me essentially for saving his life," she said. "I joined the Marine Corps to support the Marines on the ground, and to know that I succeeded in doing that is the greatest reward that I could ever ask for."

LORI HILL:
INTO HARM'S WAY

LORI HILL

Chief Warrant Officer 3 Lori Hill refused to back down. On March 21, 2006, she was piloting her Kiowa Warrior helicopter as part of a convoy security mission in Iraq when she learned that a nearby command center was under attack. She and a second helicopter were on their way to help when the enemy began to bombard their aircraft with rocket-propelled grenades and machine gun fire.

Hill swooped closer to the action to draw fire away from the lead helicopter. A rocket-propelled grenade exploded near her aircraft, damaging the transmission and hydraulics, but Hill stayed in the fight so that crew could fire down at the enemy until the American troops could reach safety.

On the third pass, a round of machine gun fire hit Hill and shattered one of her ankles. With the soldiers on the ground secure, she headed for a nearby operating base. The damage to the helicopter meant that the aircraft could not hover. Despite her painful injury, Hill performed an emergency landing, saving her crew and aircraft.

In recognition of her heroism, Hill was awarded the Distinguished Flying Cross in October 2006. She was the first woman in military history to receive the award. "Women can not only be in the military, but they can do in the military whatever they set their minds to do," Hill said in a 2017 interview.

In addition to her service in Iraq, Hill served in Germany and Korea as a pilot and aviation safety officer. After joining the military to get money for college, Hill was deployed in Operations Desert Shield and Desert Storm, as well as Operation Iraqi Freedom. She retired from the army in 2007.

Vice President Dick Cheney pins the Distinguished Flying Cross on Chief Warrant Officer 3 Lori Hill in October 2006.

PATRICIA D. HOROHO:
AMERICA'S MEDICAL EXPERT

PATRICIA D. HOROHO

In the moments after a jet crashed into the Pentagon on September 11, 2001, Lieutenant General Patricia Horoho took action. During the aftermath of the attack, she rushed to the scene and began administering medical care to those in need. That morning, she gave first aid to seventy-five victims of the terrorist attack.

That take-charge attitude is part of what allowed Horoho to hold almost every leadership position in the army's medical department, including the top job: surgeon general of the army. When Horoho became the forty-third surgeon general in 2011 under President Barack Obama, she became the first woman and the first nurse to hold the appointment.

"[Horoho has] earned this extremely important leadership position, not only because

Lieutenant General Patricia Horoho served as the forty-third surgeon general of the army. She had previously commanded the Army Nurse Corps and served in Afghanistan.

of her incredible past performance and achievements, but more importantly her outstanding potential," said army chief of staff General Raymond T. Odierno in 2011, "as she will lead Medical Command and lead as the Army surgeon general."

Patricia Dallas was born into a military family at Fort Bragg, North Carolina, in 1960. She earned her degree in nursing from the University of North Carolina at Chapel Hill in 1982, followed by a master's degree as a clinical trauma nurse specialist from the University of Pittsburgh in 1992. She followed family tradition and joined the military, rising through the ranks during her career.

Her dedication and coolheadedness in difficult situations has been clear throughout her career. She was the head nurse at Womack Army Medical Center, North Carolina, in 1994 when two aircraft crashed into each other over a landing field nearby in an accident known as the Green Ramp disaster. The injured were taken to her hospital, and Horoho managed their medical care. Twenty-four members of the army's Eighty-Second Airborne Division were killed and dozens more were injured.

Horoho displayed the same leadership during the September 11 disaster. The American Red Cross honored her as a Nurse Hero for her service on that day. "We could not be more proud of our medical team—reserves, guardsmen and civilians—who have shown such dedication to supporting our war fighters and their families," Horoho said on the tenth anniversary of the attack.

She has also received a number of military awards for service as a nurse and commander, including the Distinguished Service Medal, Bronze Star Medal, the Order of Military Medical Merit, Legion of Merit, Meritorious Service Medal, Army Commendation Medal, Army Achievement Medal, and the President's Lifetime Achievement Award.

Horoho served as surgeon general from 2011 to 2015. She is married to retired colonel Ray Horoho and they have two children. She retired from the army on February 1, 2016, after a thirty-three-year military career.

MICHELLE J. HOWARD:
REDEFINING THE ROLE OF WOMEN IN THE NAVY

MICHELLE J. HOWARD

Admiral Michelle Howard ran into a problem when she called the supplier to order a new insignia for her dress white uniform: She was told the military didn't make four-star women's shoulder boards because there had never been a female four-star admiral in the navy before.

Howard wasn't surprised. She was used to breaking new ground. She became the first female four-star admiral in the 239-year history of the navy when she was promoted in 2014. Before that, she was the first female to achieve three-star rank and before that she was the first to earn two stars. She was also the first African American woman to command a navy ship and the first female four-star admiral to command operational forces.

Admiral Michelle J. Howard became the first four-star admiral in the navy in 2014. When she was promoted, Navy Secretary Ray Mabus said her promotion is a "representation of how far we have come, and how far [Howard] has helped bring us."

STARRING ADMIRAL HOWARD AND CAPTAIN PHILLIPS

In 2009, three days after taking charge of a multinational task force on fighting piracy in the Indian Ocean, Howard was put to the test. A group of Somali pirates kidnapped Captain Richard Phillips in the Gulf of Aden and took possession of his cargo ship, and she had to put together a team and come up with a plan for his rescue. This was the first time an American flag vessel had been seized by pirates since 1821. The operation became the subject of the 2013 film *Captain Phillips*, starring Tom Hanks. Although she does not appear in the film, the movie includes a radio conversation with "Admiral Howard."

Michelle Janine Howard was born April 30, 1960, at March Air Force Base, California. Her father was an air force master sergeant. When she was twelve years old, Howard began considering a career in the military because of her admiration of her father. The military academies had opened to females just two years before Howard applied. When she entered the Naval Academy in 1978, she was one of only seven African American women in a class of 1,363 students. She graduated from the Naval Academy in 1982 and from the Army's Command and General Staff College in 1998 with a master's degree in military arts and sciences.

After leaving the Naval Academy, Howard served on the USS *Hunley* from 1982 to 1985 and then the aircraft carrier USS *Lexington* from 1985 to 1987. As she gained experience, she rose in the ranks, serving as chief engineer of the USS *Mount Hood*, first lieutenant of the USS *Flint*, and executive officer of the USS *Tortuga*. When she took command of the USS *Rushmore* in 1999 she became the first African American woman to command a ship in the navy.

In 2007, Howard was promoted to rear admiral (lower half), a one-star admiral. In 2010, she became a rear admiral; in 2012, a vice admiral; and in 2014, she was promoted to four-star admiral. She served as deputy director of the Expeditionary Warfare Division, senior military assistant to the secretary of the navy, chief of staff to the director for Strategic Plans and Policy, among other posts.

Howard also became the first female four-star admiral to command operational forces when she assumed command of U.S. Naval Forces Europe and U.S. Naval Forces Africa in 2016.

During her career, Howard has won numerous awards, including the Defense Distinguished Service Medal, Navy Distinguished Service Medal, Legion of Merit, Meritorious Service Medal, Navy and Marine Corps Commendation Medal, Navy Unit Commendation Medal, Humanitarian Service Medal, and NATO Medal, among many others. She was the 2011 United Services Organizations' Military Woman of the Year.

In an interview with the *New York Times* in 2014 Howard reflected on the expanding opportunities for women in the navy that she has witnessed during her career. "I didn't know it was possible to grow up to be anything more than a one-star," she said. Today, sailors "have never known a life when there hasn't been a woman admiral, women three-stars, women in command of ships, women in command of destroyers."

Howard remembered the challenges facing women early in her career. In 2016, she recalled a time in the 1980s when a group of female officers on an aircraft carrier asked her to confront a new captain about his antifemale behavior. Howard worried that if she spoke to him he might hold it against her; she did it anyway and found that he was, in fact, willing to listen to her remarks. "I thought if I didn't have the courage to talk to the captain, how will I ever have the courage to lead sailors into battle." Howard didn't back down, practicing the kind of leadership she was to exhibit throughout her thirty-five-year military career.

Howard retired from the navy in 2018.

DARLENE ISKRA:
THE OPPORTUNE MOMENT

DARLENE ISKRA

Darlene Iskra chose an opportune time to launch her military career: she served in the navy from 1979 to 2000, during a period when opportunities for women were expanding. She made history in 1990 when she became the first woman to command a navy ship, the USS *Opportune*.

"I hadn't realized what a big deal being the first woman to command a ship would be until I arrived in Naples, and on my desk was a stack of congratulatory cards," Iskra said in an interview in 2012.

Early in her military career, Iskra became one of the first three female sailors to attend the Naval School of Diving and Salvage. The center, the largest diving facility in the world,

Commander Darlene Iskra shortly after her appointment as commanding officer
of the USS *Opportune*, making her the first woman to be assigned
to command a navy ship.

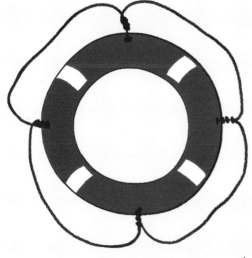

trains divers to salvage or recover ships after shipwreck or damage. After completing the program, she worked on a team that did underwater repairs and hull inspections on navy ships.

A few years into her service, Darlene learned that the navy was opening more doors for women to serve on board military ships. "Once they opened the ships, I realized that someday I could become commander of one," she said.

Iskra, who was born in 1952, was very aware that she was a role model to other women. "I knew I was the first (woman) and I felt a responsibility to show that equal opportunity works in the Navy," she said.

"All the men had ever seen women do in the past was either be nurses or administrative personnel," Iskra said. "Now, suddenly, you had women who were going to sea, going into diving, women who were flying airplanes. Those women had to work hard to build trust and prove themselves. Unfortunately, for a woman, it just seemed like every time you moved to a new command, you had to [prove yourself] again and again and again. That was the hard part."

After twenty-one years of service in the navy, Iskra retired and returned to school, earning a master's and doctorate in sociology from the University of Maryland. She taught and wrote several books about women in the military.

"The Navy changed my life," Iskra said. "It gave my life purpose and sense of honor.... Everything was new, including women serving on ships!"

THE NAVY FLEET

The navy fleet includes about 430 ships in a variety of sizes designed to do different jobs.

- **Aircraft carriers** are warships that function as mobile air bases. They have a flight deck big enough to allow aircraft to take off and land.
- **Amphibious warfare ships** support ground force attacks on land and at sea. They are often equipped with helicopters.
- **Cruisers** are warships that are smaller than battleships but larger than destroyers.
- **Destroyers** are fast-moving warships designed to defend against torpedo boats.
- **Frigates** are smaller than destroyers. They are designed to defend other ships.
- **Littoral combat ships** are smaller ships that can get closer to shore than many other ships.
- **Mine countermeasure vessels** are ships designed to find and destroy naval mines.
- **Patrol boats** are smaller vessels that are often used in coastal defense duties.
- **Submarines** are watercraft that operate underwater.

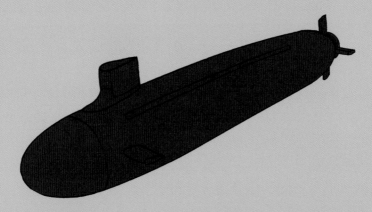

SHOSHANA JOHNSON:
STILL STANDING

When Specialist Shoshana Johnson enlisted in the army, she never expected to see combat. She signed up to be a cook! When she deployed to Iraq in 2003, she was a Quartermaster Corps food service specialist, tasked with making meals for nearly one hundred soldiers serving with the 507th Maintenance Company. But everything changed one month after she arrived to help with Operation Iraqi Freedom.

SHOSHANA JOHNSON

On March 23, 2003, Johnson was in a supply convoy of about 600 trucks driving near the city of Nasiriyah. Her truck was ambushed.

"We heard shots and suddenly we were surrounded," Johnson said in an interview with *Essence* magazine. "Our vehicle ran off the road. We scrambled for cover and hid underneath the truck so we could return fire. I got off one round and then my gun jammed. All of our weapons jammed because of the sand, so we had no way to return fire. Then I felt a burning sensation in my legs. I knew I had been hit."

A bullet had broken a bone in her left leg before passing through and severing the Achilles tendon in her right foot. She couldn't stand or walk.

Johnson and five other soldiers were captured. Specialist Shoshana Johnson became the first African American female prisoner of war in United States history.

At first, Johnson was kicked and beaten with the butt of a rifle, but the enemy stopped attacking her when they realized that she was a woman. When her captors asked what she was doing in Iraq, she said she was there to cook.

Five of the soldiers, including Johnson, were taken to Baghdad and paraded through the streets. Mobs of angry people surrounded the truck she was riding in and began to shake it back and forth while they yelled angry words in Arabic.

On April 13, 2003—after twenty-two days of being held prisoner—the United States Marines rescued Johnson and the other POWs. The hostages were welcomed home as heroes on April 16, and Johnson was able to see her two-year-old daughter again.

Shoshana Nyree Johnson calls herself Panamanian American rather than African American because she was born in Panama on January 18, 1973. A number of her family members have served in the United States military, including her father (a retired drill sergeant and veteran of the First Gulf War), her aunt (an air force nurse), her uncle (a Vietnam veteran), her sister (an army lieutenant), and several cousins. Johnson moved to the United States with her family when she was a child.

In high school, Johnson participated in the Junior Reserve Officers' Training Program. She left University of Texas at El Paso to enlist in the military in September 1998. In 2003, she was deployed to Iraq to prepare food for the mechanics who worked on the Patriot missile trucks.

On December 12, 2003, Johnson left the army with an honorable discharge. She was awarded the Bronze Star Medal, Purple Heart, and the Prisoner of War Medal for her service in Iraq.

In 2010, Johnson wrote her memoir, *I'm Still Standing: From Captive U.S. Soldier to Free Citizen—My Journey Home*. In the book she pays tribute to the eleven soldiers killed in the attack, including her close friend Private First Class Lori Ann Piestewa, the first Native American woman killed in combat. (See page 189.)

While she is still haunted by the memories of being held prisoner, she told CNN in 2015 that the experience has made her grateful for the life she leads today. "I think I'm a stronger person," Johnson said. "Things don't bother me as much, you know? Quite frankly, I'm just so very happy to be still on this earth."

KATHLEEN MCGRATH:
AYE, AYE, MA'AM

KATHLEEN MCGRATH

When Captain Kathleen McGrath took the helm of the frigate USS *Jarrett* in 1998, she became the first woman to command a ship designed for naval warfare. This was no small responsibility: The *Jarrett* was a monster—a 453-foot-long guided-missile frigate, equipped with two torpedo launchers, two helicopters, and a 262-member crew. The missiles on board had the ability to destroy enemy aircraft from twenty miles away.

Captain McGrath commanded the ship in the Persian Gulf, where the crew hunted boats suspected of smuggling Iraqi oil in violation of United Nations sanctions.

Like many other pioneering women of the military, McGrath grew up in a military family. Kathleen Anne McGrath was born on June 4, 1952, in Columbus, Ohio. She spent part of her

During her career, Captain Kathleen Anne McGrath was honored with the Legion of Merit, three Navy Commendation Medals, and four Meritorious Service Medals, among other honors.

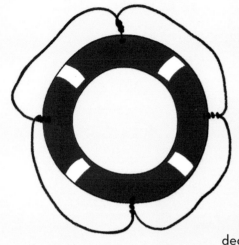

childhood at the military base in Guam while her father, an air force pilot, flew B-52 bombers over North Vietnam. McGrath graduated from California State University at Sacramento in 1975 and then worked in the U.S. Forestry Service.

In 1980, she decided to join the military. She went to visit an air force recruiter, but when she stopped by the office the air force representative was out to lunch. The navy recruiter was still on duty, so she listened to his appeal and before the air force representative returned McGrath had decided to become a sailor. The navy recruiter told McGrath she would have a chance to travel abroad. He was right: during her time in the navy, McGrath deployed to the Western Pacific, the Persian Gulf, and the Mediterranean and Caribbean seas.

Over the years, McGrath steadily took on more responsibility. In 1993 she took command of the rescue and salvage ship USS *Recovery*. Five years later, she was given command of the *Jarrett*.

In her position as commander, McGrath had the confidence to lead her own way, without trying to be tougher than her male coworkers. "I don't try to emulate a man, nor do I try to do what a guy would do," she said in an interview with *Time* magazine. "I have to be myself."

McGrath died on September 26, 2002, at age fifty from lung cancer.

In 2015, the *Jarrett* was decommissioned, dismantled, and recycled.

LINDA MCTAGUE:
IN COMMAND

LINDA MCTAGUE

Linda Kay McTague never dreamed of becoming a pilot and joining the military. She enjoyed sports, and she had studied to become a teacher. At the time she joined the air force in 1981, she had been on an airplane only once before, in college. Still, she enlisted and went through flight training school. "I did flight training in a Cessna 172 and a light went off," she said. "I realized I kind of liked flying."

From that point forward, she soared. She was stationed at Randolph Air Force Base in San Antonio, where she flew dignitaries and members of Congress around the country. "That's when I fell in love with the military," she said.

When McTague joined the air force, women weren't allowed to fly combat aircraft. She

Brigadier General Linda McTague earned a number of honors during her career, including the Legion of Merit and the Meritorious Service Medal, among others.

spent four years teaching at the Air Force Academy, and she also served as the pilot for the air force parachute team, the Wings of Blue. She then accepted a position as a pilot at the Air National Guard at Andrews Air Force Base, eventually becoming the first female commander of the District of Columbia Air National Guard's airlift squadron in 1997. In 2003, she became the first woman to assume command of an Air National Guard Wing and an air force fighter squadron.

In a 2004 interview with the air force, McTague was asked about what kind of leader she wanted to be. "I want to be a good listener," she said. "I want to try to find the niche where everybody will fit and contribute. I want to give people the opportunity to fulfill their personal goals." She said she didn't see herself as a pioneer; she said she was just "in the right place at the right time" to benefit from changing attitudes about women in the military.

After twenty-eight years of military service, McTague retired as a brigadier general in 2009. She returned home to Battle Creek, Michigan, where she had been born on November 22, 1957. In retirement she volunteered with Honor Flight, a nonprofit group that arranged for World War II veterans to travel to Washington, DC. "We really appreciate their service and this is a way to say 'thank you,'" she said in a 2014 interview with the *Coloradoan*.

McTague died in a motorcycle accident on May 10, 2017, at age fifty-nine.

MARCELLA HAYES NG:
THE FIRST AFRICAN AMERICAN PILOT

MARCELLA HAYES NG

Marcella Hayes Ng didn't set out to make history. In fact, she didn't realize that she was going to become the first African American woman pilot in the U.S. armed forces until after she had already started her training.

Marcella Anne Hayes was born on July 24, 1956, in Mexico, Missouri. She grew up climbing trees, playing tackle football, and watching her grandfather work on cars. "I grew up as a kid with rose-color glasses," she said. "The sky was always the limit."

She was raised by her grandparents and graduated from high school in Columbia, Missouri, in 1974. She attended the University of Wisconsin–Madison and joined ROTC during her second semester. She was chosen for the Tri-Service ROTC Exhibition Drill Team and excelled in leadership at ROTC Advanced Camp at Fort Riley, Kansas, in the summer of 1977. Hayes was chosen Distinguished Military Graduate in the Regular Army.

After graduating in 1978, Hayes joined the army and decided to become a pilot based on her aptitude test. On November 27, 1979, she completed her helicopter flight training at the U.S. Army Aviation Center in Fort Rucker, Alabama.

"Women were no longer separate," she said, "we were regular army officers and there were enough minorities in my program that it did not make a difference." At the time, she didn't realize that she was on track to become the first African American female helicopter pilot in the armed forces.

She met Dennis Ng in flight school; they married and had three children. She served twenty-two years in the army, holding command positions in Korea and the United States, including the Forty-ninth Transportation Battalion at Fort Hood in Texas. She retired in 2000 as a lieutenant colonel and Corps Support Command inspector general.

DR. ANTONIA NOVELLO:
THE NATION'S DOCTOR

Antonia Novello became the first woman and the first Hispanic to serve as surgeon general of the United States.

When Antonia Coello was born on August 23, 1944, in Fajardo, Puerto Rico, she was diagnosed with a painful digestive condition. She needed surgery, but her family didn't have money for the procedure. Throughout her childhood she had to make frequent trips to the hospital to manage the condition; she finally had the corrective surgery when she was eighteen years old. Antonia vowed to become a doctor to help people so that they would not have "to wait 18 years for surgery."

Antonia's father died when she was eight years old, and she was raised by her mother. She excelled in school and graduated high school at age fifteen. She graduated from the University of Puerto Rico in Rio Piedras in 1965 and from medical school at the University of Puerto Rico in San Juan in 1970.

After medical school, Antonia married Joseph Novello, and the couple moved to the United States. Antonia became a pediatric intern at the University of Michigan Medical School. In 1973, she began a residency in pediatric nephrology (study of kidneys) at Georgetown University in Washington, DC.

In 1979, Dr. Novello joined the Public Health Service Commissioned Corps and worked at the National Institute of Arthritis, Metabolism, and Digestive Diseases of the National Institutes of Health (NIH). She wanted to learn more about public health, so she went back to school, earning a master's degree in public health from the Johns Hopkins School of Hygiene and Public Health in 1982.

Dr. Novello held various positions at the NIH before being promoted to assistant surgeon general. She served as the deputy director of the National Institute of Child Health and Human Development, where she spent a lot of time working with children suffering from AIDS. She also spent time working on a law to promote fairness in the way people are chosen to receive organ transplants. This was an issue dear to Dr. Novello; her favorite aunt died from kidney failure and she vowed to improve the system.

President George H. W. Bush appointed Dr. Novello to serve as the fourteenth surgeon general of the United States from 1990 to 1993. During her time in office, she focused on the health of women, children, and minorities.

After stepping down as surgeon general, Dr. Novello stayed in the Public Health Service and served as the United Nations Children's Fund Special Representative for Health and Nutrition. In 1996, she retired from the Public Health Service as a vice admiral. She became a visiting professor of Health Policy and Management at the Johns Hopkins School of Hygiene and Public Health. She then served as commissioner of health for the State of New York from 1999 to 2006. She has been awarded the Public Health Service Distinguished Service Medal, Outstanding Service Medal, and Commendation Medal, among other honors.

WHO'S IN CHARGE?

The surgeon general and other members of the Public Health Service aren't part of the military, but they do wear uniforms, hold rank, and serve their country. The U.S. Public Health Service Commissioned Corps is one of the seven uniformed services of the United States, along with the five branches of the military and the National Oceanic and Atmospheric Administration.

The Surgeon General of the United States Army is the senior officer of the U.S. Army Medical Department. He or she provides advice on health care matters pertaining to soldiers serving in the army and the army's health care system. The first female surgeon general of the army was Lieutenant General Patricia Horoho (see page 171).

The Surgeon General of the United States is the head of the United States Public Health Service Commissioned Corps and the federal government's spokesperson on matters of public health. He or she is nominated by the president and confirmed by the Senate. The first female surgeon general of the United States was Vice Admiral Antonia Novello, M.D. (see page 187).

LORI PIESTEWA:
FIRST NATIVE AMERICAN WOMAN KILLED IN COMBAT

Private First Class Lori Piestewa became the first Native American woman to die in combat while serving in the U.S. military and the first woman to die in the Iraq War. She and nine other members of the 507th Maintenance Company were killed by a rocket-propelled grenade during the Iraq War in an ambush in 2003. She was first taken as a prisoner of war and later died. This was the same attack that injured Specialist Shoshana Johnson (see page 179).

LORI PIESTEWA

Piestewa was a member of the Hopi tribe. She was born in Tuba City, Arizona, in 1979, and lived on the Navajo Indian Reservation. Her Hopi name was Qötsa-Hon-Mana, meaning "White Bear Girl." Her father served in the army during the Vietnam War, and her grandfather served in the army during World War II.

"We need to honor all the veterans and soldiers who put their lives on the line for us," said Percy Piestewa, Lori's mother. "If it wasn't for them, we wouldn't have the freedoms we have today and that many people take for granted. I am thankful to others who came home. We are very proud of them."

Piestewa was awarded the Purple Heart and Prisoner of War Medal. The army posthumously promoted her to specialist from private first class. In 2008, the Piestewa Peak Recreation Area in the Phoenix Mountain Preserve in Arizona was named in her honor.

CORAL WONG PIETSCH:
THE FIRST ASIAN AMERICAN GENERAL

CORAL WONG PIETSCH

oral Wong's father came to the United States from Canton, China, to open a Chinese restaurant and live the American dream. A generation later, his daughter, Coral Wong Pietsch, made history by becoming the first Asian American brigadier general in the army.

"My father used to say, 'You have to be better than me,'" Pietsch said at an army Legal Services Agency event in 2014. "My father did something I'll never have to do—leave the country of my birth in search of a better life."

Coral Wong was born in 1947 and grew up in Waterloo, Iowa. Her mother was Czech American, and Coral's ethnicity made her the target of racist comments by her classmates;

one of her teachers also made fun of her last name. She earned a bachelor's degree in theater from the College of Saint Teresa and a master's degree in drama from Marquette University before attending Catholic University Law School. She graduated from law school in 1974 and married James H. Pietsch, who was also studying law. While in law school, they were both recruited into the army Judge Advocate General's (JAG) Corps.

Coral Pietsch was commissioned into the JAG Corps in 1974 and served six years on active duty in Korea and Hawaii and then transferred to the Army Reserve. She excelled in both her civilian and her Army Reserve careers. As a reservist, Pietsch was deployed to Japan; the Philippines; Washington, DC; and Iraq. As a civilian attorney she served as deputy attorney general for the State of Hawaii for six years.

In 2001, she became the first woman to be promoted to the rank of brigadier general in the army Judge Advocate General's Corps and the first woman of Asian ancestry to be promoted to brigadier general in the army. She held positions as senior attorney and special assistant at headquarters, U.S. Army Pacific, located in Hawaii. In cooperation with the Iraqi Bar Association, she helped establish a legal aid clinic at one of Iraq's largest detention facilities; on the state level, she served as the chair of the Hawaii Civil Rights Commission.

On November 1, 2011, President Barack Obama nominated Pietsch to the United States Court of Appeals for Veterans Claims. "I know what it is like to serve in a combat zone and I know what it is like to have a family member in harm's way," she said in her opening statement to the Senate Committee on Veterans' Affairs when she was a nominee for judge of the Court of Appeals. "This experience has given me a much deeper appreciation for the sacrifices made by those serving our country and for the need to address the needs of those who are experiencing difficulty due to their service."

Judge Pietsch was confirmed by the Senate in 2012, and she currently serves today. Her term expires in 2027.

LORI ROBINSON:
"I HAPPEN TO BE A WOMAN"

LORI ROBINSON

Most Americans don't know her name, but they benefit from her service every day. Air force general Lori Robinson—the highest-ranking woman in American military history—leads the U.S. Northern Command, working with homeland security and other programs to defend the United States and its allies. She is also responsible for the aerospace and maritime warning systems in the defense of North America.

"It is an honor," said General Robinson in 2016 at the ceremony when she took over the Northern Command. "I can't think of a more sacred responsibility than defense of the homeland."

Robinson was chosen for the position not because she was a woman but because she was the best person for the job. "She was selected because she was the most qualified officer," said Defense Secretary Ash Carter, who attended the ceremony at Peterson Air Force Base in Colorado when Robinson was promoted. "I hope that the excellence she represents is an inspiration to women to join our armed forces."

Robinson comes from an air force family. Her father, George Howard, was a pilot in the Vietnam War and a thirty-year air force veteran. Her husband, retired air force major general David Robinson, was a pilot with the Thunderbirds, the air force demonstration team.

Robinson was born January 27, 1959, in Big Spring, Texas. She graduated from the

General Lori Robinson became the most powerful woman in the military when she took command of the United States Northern Command and North American Aerospace Defense Command in 2016.

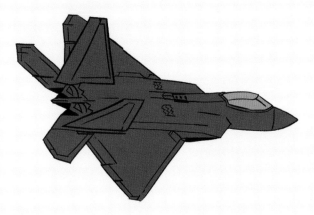

University of New Hampshire in 1982 and was commissioned as a second lieutenant in the air force. Four years later, she became the first female instructor at the Air Force Fighter Weapons School at Nellis Air Force Base, Nevada. Step by step, she steadily rose through the ranks, becoming a brigadier general in 2008.

Many have described Robinson as part of a new generation of leaders in the air force who recognize the importance of space, cybersecurity, and the use of drones, in addition to traditional flying and fighting.

Robinson doesn't dwell on the fact that she is the first woman to lead a major fighting command. "I often say to people, 'I'm the commander of Pacific Air Forces, I'm a general in the United States Air Force, I'm an airman, and I happen to be a woman,'" she said. Before taking over the Northern Command, Robinson was commander of the Pacific Air Forces in Hawaii, making her the first female four-star commander of combat forces.

While Robinson was not the first or the only female four-star general, the responsibility required of her assignment makes her the most powerful woman in the military. Her personal decorations include the Air Battle Manager Badge, Defense Distinguished Service Medal, Air Force Distinguished Service Medal, Defense Superior Service Medal, Legion of Merit, Bronze Star Medal, and Defense Meritorious Service Medal, among others.

ANGELA SALINAS:
"SOMETHING GREATER THAN MYSELF"

ANGELA SALINAS

Angela Salinas grew up watching news about the Vietnam War on television every night, but she didn't think that the military had anything to do with her. She had seen plenty of Marine Corps recruitment posters and she knew their slogan—"The Marines are looking for a few good men"—but again, the message didn't seem directed at her. That changed one day when Salinas was walking into a post office as a college sophomore on the verge of dropping out of school: a marine recruiter stopped and asked, "Why aren't you a Marine?"

At first, she couldn't imagine herself as a marine. By the time she retired as the first Hispanic female major general in the Marine Corps thirty-nine years later, she couldn't imagine herself in any other way.

Angela Salinas was born on December 6, 1953, in Alice, Texas. She was the youngest of five children in a family that had been living in Texas for generations. Her father was a mechanic and her mother a housekeeper. Angela became the first member of her family to go to college, but she did not thrive in her studies as a history major at Dominican University of California. She considered dropping out and she wasn't sure about her future. When the recruiter approached her, Salinas was open to considering a future with the Marine Corps.

In May 1974, Salinas enlisted. "It ignited in me a passion to do something greater than myself," she said. "I knew, looking around, there weren't (marines) who looked like me, but it wasn't until years later that being a Latina as well meant so much."

Salinas initially thought she would serve for a short period of time, but she loved the people she was working with. "It's a special breed of people who raise their hands and say, 'I do solemnly swear that I will support and defend the Constitution of the United States against all enemies, foreign and domestic; that I will bear true faith and allegiance to the same,'" she said. "The Corps' values are honor, courage, commitment. You're serving something greater than yourself."

Salinas served in a time that the armed forces were making an effort to provide broader opportunities for women. In 1977, she was chosen to attend the Enlisted Commissioning Program; she was commissioned as a second lieutenant after graduating from Dominican University of San Rafael.

During her time in the military, Salinas commanded at every rank. She often worked with military recruitment, and in 1988 she became the first woman to command a recruiting station when she operated the Recruiting Station Charleston. In 1992 she became the first woman assigned as a combat support ground monitor and she was responsible for the assignment of more than 1,000 senior officers. Her responsibilities changed as she was promoted steadily throughout her career.

In 2006, she was promoted to brigadier general, becoming the first Hispanic woman to hold that rank. She assumed command of Marine Corps Recruit Depot San Diego. Four years later she was promoted again to major general.

During her career she earned the Navy Distinguished Service Medal, Defense Superior Service Medal, Legion of Merit, Meritorious Service Medal, Navy and Marine Corps Commendation Medal, Army Commendation Medal, and the Navy and Marine Corps Achievement Medal. She holds a master's degree from the Naval War College, and she is a graduate of Amphibious Warfare School, Naval War College's Command and Staff College, and the Army War College.

In 2013, she retired after thirty-nine years of service as the highest-ranking female in the Marine Corps.

SANDRA STOSZ:
THE STUDENT BECOMES THE TEACHER

SANDRA STOSZ

During Sandra Stosz's junior year of high school, a neighbor brought her a newspaper article that explained that the naval academies were going to start accepting women. She was intrigued. "I remember thinking about all the cool things you could do there and it said they would give you a stipend," she said. "I had to look up the word in the dictionary to see what a stipend was."

Stosz applied and was accepted to the Coast Guard Academy in New London, Connecticut, in 1978, two years after women were first admitted. Thirty-three years later, in 2011, she was in charge: she served as the first female superintendent of the Coast Guard Academy, making her the first women to lead a U.S. service academy.

Stosz was born in 1960 and grew up in Takoma Park, Maryland, where she was a high school all-American in the discus and a Junior Olympic swimmer. When she attended the Coast Guard Academy she had to compete on boys' sports teams because a women's sports program hadn't been developed yet.

"I was the only female in some of my classes," Stosz said, recalling what it was like to be one of the first women to go through the academy. Thirty female cadets started the program, and she was one of twelve who stuck it out and earned her ensign stripes as a graduate in 1982.

Stosz continued to distinguish herself during her career. In 1990, she became the first woman to command a coast guard cutter when she served on the USCGC *Katmai Bay*, a 140-foot ice-breaking tug with a crew of seventeen stationed in the Great Lakes. (A cutter is a commissioned ship sixty-five feet or longer.) She took on positions with the Coast Guard Reserve, in addition to programs at the coast guard headquarters.

While in the coast guard, Stosz served twelve years at sea, including duty on board two heavy icebreakers and command of two cutters. She and her crews executed many types of missions, including search and rescue, icebreaking, ports and waterway security, and law enforcement.

Stosz served as superintendent of the Coast Guard Academy from 2011 to 2015. She was the first woman to do so. In her change-of-command speech when leaving her position at the academy, she said, "I don't see this so much as a milestone but rather a natural progression in the coast guard's efforts to create a climate of equity and inclusion."

In 2015, Stosz was promoted to vice admiral and began serving in Washington, DC, as deputy commandant for mission support. She retired in 2018.

Her personal awards include the Coast Guard Distinguished Service Medal, three Legion of Merit Medals, four Meritorious Service Medals, two Coast Guard Commendation Medals, and two Coast Guard Achievement Medals.

NADJA WEST:
"I COULDN'T WAIT TO SIGN UP"

NADJA WEST

When she was two years old, Nadja West was adopted. Her new father was a career soldier living outside Washington, DC, who taught his twelve adopted children that the United States is the greatest country in the world. "And it is," West said in an interview with the *Journal of the Student National Medical Association*. Where else could an orphaned child grow up to become the first African American woman three-star general and the first black surgeon general of the army?

"I went from an orphan with an uncertain future to... leading an incredible organization of men and women in army medicine," she said in an interview with CNN. "It's very humbling."

As a child, West was inspired by seeing the black, female character Uhura in a position

"One characteristic that stands out in all the leaders I've seen is empathy," West said. "You don't have to be like everyone else, but you can try to connect with other people."

of authority on the television show *Star Trek*, but she wanted to be Spock, the science officer. After finishing high school, West applied to the United States Military Academy at West Point, which had recently begun accepting women. "I couldn't wait to sign up," West said. "I thought it was what you were supposed to do."

She graduated from West Point in 1982 and the George Washington University School of Medicine in 1988. She completed her family medicine internship and residency at Martin Army Hospital, in Fort Benning, Georgia, and her residency in dermatology at Fitzsimons Army Medical Center and the University of Colorado Medical Center. She deployed during Operation Desert Storm and Operation Desert Shield.

In 2013, West was promoted to major general, and two years later she was promoted to lieutenant general. She also became the forty-fourth army surgeon general and the first African American woman to fill the position.

"If you told me when I was a plebe at West Point that [I would become] a three-star general, I would have laughed you out of the room because . . . I couldn't see it in myself," West said in an interview with CNN.

When asked about her promotion to lieutenant general, West told a reporter with the Student National Medical Association: "My parents taught me to work hard and be the best I can be and things will work out . . . We all want to see people who look like us doing certain things to give us inspiration. Hopefully, I can inspire someone to be able to say, 'I can do that.'"

Her awards include the Army Distinguished Service Medal, the Legion of Merit, Defense Superior Service Medal, Defense Meritorious Service Medal, Army Commendation Medal, Army Achievement Medal, NATO Medal for Former Yugoslavia, and the Army Parachutist Badge, among others. She is a Fellow of the American Academy of Dermatology and the American Academy of Family Physicians.

SHEILA WIDNALL:
HEAD OF THE AIR FORCE

Sheila Widnall was a member of the board of investigation into the space shuttle *Columbia* disaster.

The military is made up of soldiers, but it is controlled by civilians. The ultimate authority lies with the president of the United States, the commander in chief, who is responsible for all final military decisions. The secretary of the Department of Defense reports to the president and has control over the branches of the military, except the coast guard, which is under the Department of Homeland Security. (In wartime, the coast guard comes under the command of the navy.) Each branch of the military is controlled by a civilian secretary, who is appointed by the president and approved by Congress.

Sheila Marie Evans Widnall became the first woman to lead a branch of the military when she took over as secretary of the air force in 1993.

Widnall spent most of her career as an academic. She was born in 1938 and graduated from the Massachusetts Institute of Technology (MIT) with an undergraduate degree in aeronautics and astronautics in 1960. She received her master's degree the following year and her doctorate in 1964. She spent more than two decades as a faculty member at MIT, teaching aeronautics and mathematics. She served as chairwoman of the Air Force Academy's board of visitors from 1980 to 1982 and on several air force advisory boards.

In 1993, Widnall was nominated to be secretary of the air force by President Bill Clinton. She was approved by Congress and served from 1993 to 1997, making her the first woman to lead an entire branch of the U.S. military. She returned to MIT when she left the air force.

"I think she's had an enormous impact on women in the military," said Sheila Cheston, general counsel of the Department of the Air Force in an interview with CNN. "By virtue of being not only a woman, but an extremely qualified woman in that position, she has broken a barrier and she sends a loud and clear message to women throughout the military about what is possible."

JANET WOLFENBARGER:
FOUR STARS IN THE AIR FORCE

JANET WOLFENBARGER

When Janet Carol Libby Wolfenbarger joined the air force in 1980, about 10 percent of the people serving were women. Today, that number has climbed to about 20 percent. "We're not done," said Wolfenbarger, who became the first four-star general in the air force in 2012. "Twenty percent is not representative of demographics of this country and so we continue to embrace programs that will allow us to attract and retain women for our United States Air Force."

Wolfenbarger's career shows that there are opportunities for women to soar through the ranks in the air force. She was born in Tampa, Florida, in 1958, and graduated from the Air Force Academy in 1980. She spent much of her career involved with acquisition of weapons and aircraft. She returned to school and earned a master's degree in aeronautics and astronautics from MIT in 1985 and another master's in national resource strategy from the Industrial College of the Armed Forces in 1994.

In 2012, President Barack Obama nominated Wolfenbarger to serve as the first female four-star general in the air force. The Senate confirmed the appointment and she became the highest-ranking woman in the air force on March 26, 2012. In an interview with the *Air Force Times*, Wolfenbarger said she has "learned and grown from every opportunity that my Air Force has given me."

Still, her success in the air force exceeded her expectations. "Never would have expected that I would make one-star, much less four," Wolfenbarger said in an interview with the *New York Times*.

From 2012 to 2015, Wolfenbarger served as commander of the Air Force Materiel Command, meaning she handled equipment and weapons acquisitions for the air force.

Wolfenbarger retired from the air force in July 2015 after more than thirty-five years of service. Her major military awards include the Air Force Distinguished Service Medal, Legion of Merit, Meritorious Service Medal, Air Force Commendation Medal, Air Force Achievement Medal, and Global War on Terrorism Service Medal, among other honors. She accepted a volunteer position as chair of the Defense Advisory Committee on Women in the Services. The committee offers advice and recommendations on issues involving recruitment, retention, and treatment of women in the armed forces. The future success of the military depends on providing equal opportunities for all recruits, regardless of sex.

EPILOGUE

Throughout American history, women have been part of the U.S. military. The women included in this book—as well as hundreds of thousands of others who have not been mentioned by name—have voluntarily served and sacrificed for their country's defense.

Their service speaks for itself: more than two hundred years of history have demonstrated that women are willing and able to participate in all branches of the armed forces. Women have done what has been asked of them—everything from nursing the sick to flying fighter planes to leading their fellow soldiers in battle. Women make the military stronger, and by making the military stronger, they make America stronger, safer, and more secure.

As the various branches of the armed services have opened more positions of responsibility to females, women have been able to demonstrate their skills as they have put their patriotism into action. The armed forces should employ the best-qualified soldiers, whether female or male. These service members should be chosen based on ability and performance: They should be smart, dedicated, proud, and willing to love and serve their country.

The modern military relies more than ever before on the development and use of advanced technology. Today, a well-trained soldier can use her skills and know-how to serve her country by programming drones, directing cyberspace operations, analyzing geospatial data, operating satellite communications equipment, maintaining Patriot launch stations, and performing dozens of other high-tech jobs. In addition, 2018 saw a record number of women veterans running for, being elected to, and serving in Congress. Women like Martha McSally (air force), Elaine Luria (navy), Mikie Sherrill (navy), Chrissy Houlahan (air force), Amy McGrath (Marine Corps), and Gina Ortiz Jones (air force). These women join the other female veterans, such as Tammy Duckworth and Joni Ernst, already serving in Congress. In all these positions, intellect and training matter; brute strength and gender do not.

On the ground, women have also shown that they can be integral members of

combat battalions in the modern military. Even before the Pentagon officially allowed women to fight, some had already served on the battlefield because they had been assigned as intelligence and communications officers with combat units. In her 2013 book *Undaunted: The Real Story of America's Servicewomen in Today's Military*, Tanya Biank wrote about women finally being allowed to serve in combat. "It was like finally giving a team jersey to a player who had been hitting home runs on the field for years."

Why do women serve in the military? The answer, of course, depends on the individual. For the most part, they serve for the same reasons men do: because they love their country and feel a patriotic duty to protect it, because they want to get a good education or technical training and they need assistance paying for school, and because they envision a meaningful and successful career in the armed services. For some, military service is a family tradition; others want to be the first in their family to put on a uniform and serve. Some women long for adventure; others long for the security

offered by a career in the military.

In the future, women will assume more top leadership roles in the military. A time will come when women's right to serve will not be questioned, and society will no longer take special note of a female being promoted to four-star general or serving as a commander in the navy or air force. And someday—when a woman is finally elected president of the United States—she will serve in the ultimate seat of military authority, as commander in chief of the armed forces.

WORDS TO LIVE BY

These are some of the best-known military mottos of the armed forces.

Air Force: "Aim high . . . fly-fight-win"

Army: "This we'll defend"

Army National Guard: "You can"

Army Rangers: *"Sua sponte"* (Rangers lead the way!)

Coast Guard: *"Semper paratus"* (Always ready)

1st Marine Division: "No better friend, no worse enemy"

Marine Corps: *"Semper fidelis"* (Always faithful)

National Guard: "Always ready, always there"

Navy: *"Non sibi sed patriae"* (Not self, but country)

Navy SEALs: "The only easy day was yesterday"

TIMELINE

1775–1783	**REVOLUTIONARY WAR**
1775	Continental Army, Navy, Marines established
1783	Continental Army disbanded
1784	First American Regiment created
1790	Coast Guard established
1794	Naval Act creates American navy
1798	Marine Corps becomes independent branch of military
1812	**WAR OF 1812**
1846–1848	**MEXICAN-AMERICAN WAR**
1861–1865	**AMERICAN CIVIL WAR**
1898	**SPANISH-AMERICAN WAR**
1901	Army Nurse Corps established
1908	Navy Nurse Corps established
1914–1918	**WORLD WAR I**
1917	United States enters World War I
1917	First American females die serving in the military
1918	First woman enlists in non-nursing position
1939–1945	**WORLD WAR II**
Dec. 7, 1941	Japan bombs Pearl Harbor, Hawaii
1942	Women's Army Auxiliary Corps (WAAC) established
1942	Women's Auxiliary Ferrying Squadron (WAFS) established

1942	Coast Guard Women's Reserve (SPARs) established
1942	Navy Women Accepted for
	Volunteer Emergency Service
	(WAVES) established
1943	Women Airforce Service Pilots (WASP) established
1943	WAAC becomes Women's Army Corps (WAC)
1943	Marine Corps Women's Reserve established
1947	Air Force established
1948	President Harry Truman signs executive order integrating the military
1948	Congress passes Women's Armed Services Integration Act
1950–1953	**KOREAN WAR**
1955–1975	**VIETNAM WAR**
1970	First female army generals commissioned
1973	United States becomes an all-volunteer military
1990–1991	**GULF WAR**
1994	Roles of women expanded to all but combat positions
2001–PRESENT	**AFGHANISTAN WAR**
2003–2011	**IRAQ WAR**
2016	Women permitted to serve in all military jobs, including combat
2017	First women graduate from gender-integrated infantry basic training
2014–PRESENT	**IRAQI CIVIL WAR**

MILITARY RANKS

Leadership and authority are critical to the success of the military. Each branch of the military has a different system of ranking its enlisted soldiers and officers. The stripes and bars worn on the shoulders of military uniforms show a soldier's rank.

Flag Rank Officers

A flag rank officer is a commissioned officer senior enough to fly a flag to mark his or her command post.

ARMY	MARINE CORPS	NAVY/COAST GUARD	AIR FORCE
General	General	Fleet Admiral	General of the Air Force
General	General	Admiral	General
Lieutenant General	Lieutenant General	Vice Admiral	Lieutenant General
Major General	Major General	Rear Admiral (upper half)	Major General
Brigadier General	Brigadier General	Rear Admiral (lower half)	Brigadier General

Commissioned Officers

Commissioned officers are the leaders and supervisors of enlisted soldiers.

ARMY	MARINE CORPS	NAVY/COAST GUARD	AIR FORCE
Colonel	Colonel	Captain	Colonel
Lieutenant Colonel	Lieutenant Colonel	Commander	Lieutenant Colonel
Major	Major	Lieutenant Commander	Major
Captain	Captain	Lieutenant	Captain
1st Lieutenant	1st Lieutenant	Lieutenant, Junior Grade	1st Lieutenant
2nd Lieutenant	2nd Lieutenant	Ensign	2nd Lieutenant

Warrant Officers

Warrant officers hold a rank above enlisted ranks and below commissioned officers. They typically have special expertise or skills.

ARMY	MARINE CORPS	NAVY/COAST GUARD
Chief Warrant Officer, Five	Chief Warrant Officer, Five	Not in use
Chief Warrant Officer, Four	Chief Warrant Officer, Four	Chief Warrant Officer, Four
Chief Warrant Officer, Three	Chief Warrant Officer, Three	Chief Warrant Officer, Three
Chief Warrant Officer, Two	Chief Warrant Officer, Two	Chief Warrant Officer, Two
Warrant Officer, One	Warrant Officer	Not in use

Enlisted Soldiers

Enlisted soldiers carry out orders or missions. A noncommissioned officer is an enlisted member of the military with some authority.

ARMY	MARINE CORPS	NAVY/COAST GUARD	AIR FORCE
Sergeant Major	Sergeant Major	Master Chief Petty Officer	Chief Master Sergeant
Command Sergeant Major	Sergeant Major	Command Master Chief Petty Officer	Command Chief Master Sergeant
Sergeant Major	Master Gunnery Sergeant	Master Chief Petty Officer	Chief Master Sergeant
First Sergeant	First Sergeant	Senior Chief Petty Officer	First Sergeant
Master Sergeant	Master Sergeant	Senior Chief Petty Officer	Senior Master Sergeant
Sergeant First Class	Gunnery Sergeant	Chief Petty Officer	Master Sergeant
Staff Sergeant	Staff Sergeant	Petty Officer First Class	Technical Sergeant
Sergeant	Sergeant	Petty Officer Second Class	Staff Sergeant
Specialist/Corporal	Corporal	Petty Officer Third Class	Senior Airman
Private First Class	Lance Corporal	Seaman	Airman First Class
Private Second Class	Private First Class	Seaman Apprentice	Airman
Private	Private	Seaman Recruit	Airman Basic

NOTES

UNEXPECTED PATRIOTS: WOMEN IN THE REVOLUTIONARY WAR

7   *Resolved, That Margaret Corbin:* Greg Timmons, "Molly Pitcher," Teacher Resources, E-newsletter, Primary Source of the Month, Colonial Williamsburg, http://www.history.org/history/teaching/enewsletter /volume7/nov08/primsource.cfm.

11   *"She did a Soldier's duty":* Rebecca Beatrice Brooks, "Deborah Sampson: Woman Warrior of the American Revolution," *History of Massachusetts* (blog), Dec. 29, 2011, http://historyofmassachusetts.org /deborah-sampson-woman-warrior-of-the-american-revoultion/.

13   *"treasonable correspondence":* Rebecca Beatrice Brooks, "Prudence Cummings Wright & Leonard Whiting's Guard," ibid., May 13, 2013.

DON'T MESS WITH TEXAS: WOMEN IN THE MEXICAN-AMERICAN WAR

18   *"She could whip any man":* Joe Holley, "This Woman Was Worthy of Her Legendary Status," *Houston Chronicle,* June 10, 2016, https://www.houstonchronicle.com/news/columnists/native-texan/article /A-woman-worthy-of-legendary-status-8004022.php.

20   *"Heroine of Fort Brown":* ibid.

WOMEN WARRIORS: WOMEN IN THE CIVIL WAR

26   *"They fought like demons":* Brigid Schulte, "Women Soldiers Fought, Bled, and Died in the Civil War, Then Were Forgotten," *Washington Post,* April 29, 2013, https://www.washingtonpost.com/local/women -soldiers-fought-bled-and-died-in-the-civil-war-then-were-forgotten/2013/04/26/fa722dba-a1a2-11e2 -82bc-511538ae90a4_story.html?utm_term=.f89eedb93cf5.

28   *Dragon Dix:* "Dorothea Dix," National Museum of Civil War Medicine, March 14, 2016, http://www .civilwarmed.org/dorothea-dix/.

31   *"I could only thank God":* S. Emma E. Edmonds, *Nurse and Spy in the Union Army: The Adventures, Experiences of a Woman in Hospitals, Camps, and Battle-Fields* (Hartford, CT: W. S. Williams, 1865); Project Gutenberg, 2012, http://www.gutenberg.org/files/38497/38497-h/38497-h.htm.

34   *I had expected to meet an amazon:* Irishacw, "Jennie Hodgers: The Irishwoman Who Fought as a Man in the Union Army," Irish in the American Civil War, August 17, 2011, https://irishamericancivilwar.com/jennie -hodgers-the-irishwoman-who-fought-as-a-man-in-the-union-army/.

38   *"There are two things I've got a right to":* Harriet Tubman Historical Society. http://www.harriet-tubman.org /quotes/.

39   *Black Moses*: "The Black Moses," Digital History, ID 508, http://www.digitalhistory.uh.edu/disp_textbook
      .cfm?smtID=3&psid=508.

39   *I never lost a passenger*: Kate Clifford Larson, "Bound for the Promised Land: Harriet Tubman, Portrait
      of an American Hero," Harriet Tubman Myths and Facts, http://www.harriettubmanbiography.com/harriet-
      tubman-myths-and-facts.html.

41   *I don't know how long before*: "Sarah Rosetta Wakeman," Civil War Biography, American Battlefield Trust,
      https://www.civilwar.org/learn/biographies/sarah-rosetta-wakeman.

42   *I don't care anything about coming home*: "In Her Own Words: Civil War Soldier Sarah Rosetta Wakeman,"
      The Smell of Gunsmoke: Adventures in Researching and Writing Fiction Set in the Old West, Dec. 8, 2013,
      https://thesmellofgunsmoke.com/2013/12/08/sarah-rosetta-wakeman/.

44   *I don't wear men's clothes*: Anika Burgess, "The Unconventional Life of Mary Walker, the Only Woman
      to Have Received the U.S. Medal of Honor," Atlas Obscura, Sept. 27, 2017, https://www.atlasobscura.com
      /articles/mary-walker-feminist-dress-reform-equal-rights.

45   *lady physician in bloomers*: Matt Reimann, "The Only Woman to Win the Medal of Honor Fought for Her
      Role in the Civil War," Timeline, March 24, 2017, https://timeline.com/mary-edwards-walker-2b0a358ace87.

A NEW KIND OF SOLDIER:
WOMEN IN THE SPANISH-AMERICAN WAR AND WORLD WAR I

52   *Is there any law*: "The Price of Freedom: Americans at War, Object Record: Yeoman (F) Uniform," National
      Museum of American History, Smithsonian Institution, https://amhistory.si.edu/militaryhistory/collection
      /object.asp?ID=769.

57   *It is too soon as yet*: Esther V. Hasson, "The Navy Nurse Corps," *American Journal of Nursing* 9 (March
      1909): 410–15, https://www.jstor.org/stable/3402927?seq=1#page_scan_tab_contents.

61   *Anybody that calls me anything*: Petula Dvorak, "The First Woman Marine: In 1918, She Couldn't
      Vote but Rushed to Serve," *Washington Post*, Sept. 22, 2017, https://www.washingtonpost.com/news
      /retropolis/wp/2017/09/22/the-first-woman-marine-in-1918-she-couldnt-vote-but-rushed-to-serve
      /?utm_term=.74e22f4c23ba.

65   *yeomanettes or yeowomen*: William C. Kashatus, "First Active Duty Navy Woman Has Ties to Region," *Cit-
      izens' Voice*, March 22, 2015, http://citizensvoice.com/arts-living/first-active-duty-navy-woman-has-ties-to
      -region-1.1850460.

IT'S OUR WAR, TOO: WOMEN IN WORLD WAR II

69   *Free a man to fight*: Rick Huenefeld and Barbara McCurtis, "Free a Man to Fight: Marine Corps Women
      Reserve, Marine Base, San Diego, 1943–1946," Women Marines Association, Sept. 26, 2016, https://women
      -marines.wordpress.com/2016/09/26/free-a-man-to-fight/.

73   *Angels of Bataan . . . Battling Belles of Bataan*: Elizabeth M. Collins, "The 'Angels of Bataan,'" *Soldiers: The*

Official U.S. Army Magazine, http://soldiers.dodlive.mil/2012/03/the-angels-of-bataan/.

76   *"Using the camera"*: Margaret Bourke-White, *Portrait of Myself* (New York: Simon & Schuster, 1963), 259.

77   *Speed Queen*: "Jacqueline Cochran," *New World Encyclopedia*, http://www.newworldencyclopedia.org/entry/Jacqueline_Cochran.

78   *"In the field of aviation"*: "Jackie Cochran's Proposal to Eleanor Roosevelt for Women Pilots in National Emergency," Letter from Jacqueline Cochran to Eleanor Roosevelt, Sept. 28, 1939, Liberty Letters, Filing Cabinet: Pearl Harbor, http://www.libertyletters.com/resources/pearl-harbor/cochrans-letter-to-roosevelt.php.

82   *"Women have reached a situation"*: Linda Matchett, "Dr. Margaret Craighill: First of Her Kind," Stitches Thru Time, March 28, 2017, http://stitchesthrutime.blogspot.com/2017/03/dr-margaret-craighill-first-of-her-kind.html.

84   *"You will shoot"*: Erin Blakemore, "The Officer Who Opened the U.S. Navy for Asian-American Women," Time.com, May 3, 2016, http://time.com/4314308/susan-cuddy-history/.

86   *"I'm going to send a white first lieutenant: Ibid.*

88   *"When I talk to students"*: Richard Goldstein, "Charity Adams Earley: Black Pioneer in WACS, Dies at 83," *New York Times*, Jan. 22, 2002, https://www.nytimes.com/2002/01/22/us/charity-adams-earley-black-pioneer-in-wacs-dies-at-83.html.

90   *"a date which will live in infamy"*: "'A Date Which Will Live in Infamy,' The First Typed Draft of Franklin D. Roosevelt's War Address," National Archives, Educator Resources, https://www.archives.gov/education/lessons/day-of-infamy.

90   *"singularly meritorious act"*: "Women Who Served, Annie G. Fox," A People at War, National Archives and Records Administration, https://www.archives.gov/exhibits/a_people_at_war/women_who_served/annie_g_fox.html.

92   *"I was afraid"*: Pathbreakers: Joy Bright Hancock, *Lady in the Navy: A Personal Reminiscence* (Annapolis, MD: Naval Institute Press, 1972).

92   *"It would appear to me that any national defense weapon"*: https://history.army.mil/brochures/WAC/WAC.HTM

95   *"The gaps our women will fill"*: Kay Bailey Hutchison, "Women's History Month: 'Oveta Culp Hobby,'" Humanities Texas, March 2012, http://www.humanitiestexas.org/news/articles/womens-history-month-oveta-culp-hobby-senator-kay-bailey-hutchison.

98   *Dare and Do*: Rear Admiral Brian Fort, "Hopper: Innovation, Transformation, Inspiration," USS *Hopper*, America's Navy, U.S. Navy, March 21, 2018, http://www.public.navy.mil/surfor/ddg70/Pages/default.aspx#.WtqEWS-ZOi4.

104   *"I will summon every resource"*: "Nurse's Creed," National Museum of the U.S. Air Force, May 1, 2015, http://www.nationalmuseum.af.mil/Visit/Museum-Exhibits/Fact-Sheets/Display/Article/196420/flight-nurses-creed/.

105   *High Pockets:* Daniel Stashower, "The Female American Spy Who Lured Secrets from Japanese Offi-cers in WWII," *Washington Post,* June 9, 2017, https://www.washingtonpost.com/opinions/the-female-american-spy-who-lured-secrets-from-japanese-officers-in-ww-ii/2017/06/09/9c1580d8-23a2-11e7-bb9d-8cd6118e1409_story.html?noredirect=on&utm_term=.eede6fc0c08b.

108   *"I understand that all information":* Lt. Col. Mary E. V. Frank, A.N., "The Forgotten POW: Second Lieutenant Reba Z. Whittle, A.N., An Individual Study Project, U.S. Army War College, Carlisle Barracks, PA, Feb. 1, 1990, http://www.dtic.mil/dtic/tr/fulltext/u2/a223404.pdf.

HERE TO STAY: WOMEN IN THE KOREAN WAR

119   *"The Nurse Who Forgot Fear":* "Distinguished Flying Cross Recipient: Bonham, Jonita Ruth," US Mil-itaria Forum, August 20, 2014, http://www.usmilitariaforum.com/forums/index.php?/topic/217657-female-armed-forces-personnel-decorated-in-korean-war/.

121   *"They let me take the test":* Lt. Stephanie Young, "Making Waves: Capt. Eleanor L'Ecuyer, *Coast Guard Compass: Official Blog of the U.S. Coast Guard,* November 23, 2011, http://coastguard.dodlive.mil/2011/11/making-waves-capt-eleanor-lecuyer/.

123   *"not given to compromise":* Jeanne M. Holm, *Women in the Military: An Unfinished Revolution* (Novato, CA: Presidio Press, 1992).

BREAKING THE BRASS CEILING: WOMEN IN THE VIETNAM WAR

130   *"She volunteered [for the assignment in Vietnam] at a time":* James Clark, "The First Female Marine to Serve in a Combat Zone Volunteered for Vietnam," Task & Purpose, March 18, 2016, https://taskandpurpose.com/the-first-female-marine-to-serve-in-a-combat-zone-volunteered-for-vietnam/.

130   *"Women were looking":* Ibid.

131   *The first question most generally:* Jerri Bell and Tracy Crow, eds., *It's My Country Too: Women's Military Sto-ries from the American Revolution to Afghanistan* (Lincoln: University of Nebraska Press, 2017), https://books.google.com/books?id=2OYlDwAAQBAJ&pg=PT158&lpg=PT158&dq=barbara+dulinsky&source=bl&ots=ZNLWxRN9rd&sig=rwOA4qGXcT0t3dEOK2_hpFl8ZD4&hl=en&sa=X&ved=0ahUKEwiokub1mL_aAhUl7awKHYJaBFo4FBDoAQhBMAU#v=onepage&q=barbara%20dulinsky&f=false.

133   *"Each of us must not only be able to communicate":* André B. Sobocinski, "Alene Duerk: Celebrating the 98th Birthday of a Navy Icon," The Sextant: Taking a Fix on the History and Heritage of Today's U.S. Navy, March 26, 2018, http://usnhistory.navylive.dodlive.mil/2018/03/26/alene-duerk-celebrating-the-98th-birthday-of-a-navy-icon/.

134   *"The war was declared on 7 December 1941":* Jared Keller, "Anna Mae Hays, the US Military's First Female General, Dies at Age 97," Task & Purpose, January 9, 2018, https://taskandpurpose.com/anna-mae-hays-female-general/.

135   *"If you would ask me what are the first things":* ibid.

135   *"The minute she heard about the WAC"*: Matt Schudel, "Pioneering Brig. Gen. Elizabeth P. Hoisington," *Washington Post*, August 24, 2007, http://www.washingtonpost.com/wp-dyn/content/article/2007/08/23/AR2007082302337.html.

136   *"We were always just as much officers"*: ibid.

136   *"The Army is my first love"*: ibid.

138   *"I was more surprised than anyone"*: "AME minister, Rev. Alice M. Henderson, Blazes Trail for Women Clerics in the Army," *Ebony*, October 1975, 44, https://books.google.com/books?id=jw14Q2YAspMC&pg=PA44&lpg=PA44&dq=rev.+alice+henderson&source=bl&ots=-SdkxqMhoU&sig=s5rF1of-ifUOFvB_3zj2v3cnmlE&hl=en&sa=X&ved=0ahUKEwjWqq2mrr_aAhVHNd8KHdt_CrcQ6AEINDAD#v=onepage&q=rev.%20alice%20henderson&f=false.

APPROACHING EQUALITY: WOMEN IN THE MODERN MILITARY

147   *"If members of our military can meet"*: Claudette Roulo, "Defense Department Expands Women's Combat Role," American Forces Press Service, Jan. 24, 2013, http://archive.defense.gov/news/newsarticle.aspx?id=119098.

147   *"They'll be allowed to drive tanks"*: Charly Pellerin, "Carter Opens All Military Occupations, Positions to Women," Department of Defense News, Dec. 3, 2015, https://www.defense.gov/News/Article/Article/632536/carter-opens-all-military-occupations-positions-to-women/.

149   *"Quite honestly"*: W. V. Fitzgerald, "Army Trailblazer Gwendolyn Bingham Promoted to Brigadier General," *Digital Journal*, April 23, 2011, http://www.digitaljournal.com/article/305926.

150   *"Inside, she has the heart of a lion"*: ibid.

151   *"I remember sitting at my desk"*: Julie Summers Walker, "Five Questions: Eileen Collins, Retired Air Force Colonel, U.S. Astronaut," AOPA, Oct. 1, 2017, https://www.aopa.org/news-and-media/all-news/2017/october/flight-training-magazine/five-questions-eileen-collins.

152   *"I wanted to be part of our nation's"*: "Eileen Collins: NASA's First Female Shuttle Commander," NASA, Oct. 4, 2003, https://www.nasa.gov/news/highlights/Eileen_Collins.html.

156   *"You can choose to cry"*: Rebecca Nelson, "The Dark Humor of Tammy Duckworth, Iraq War Hero and Gun Control Advocate," *GQ*, Sept. 29, 2016, https://www.gq.com/story/tammy-duckworth-iraq-war-hero-and-gun-control-advocate-interview.

156   *"Alive Day"*: "Tammy Duckworth Speaks About Her 'Alive Day,'" Nov. 12, 2013, https://www.tammyduckworth.com/news/tammy-duckworth-speaks-about-her-alive-day/.

158   *"I've always had male bosses"*: C. Todd Lopez, "First Female Four-Star General Retires from Army," Army News Service, Aug. 15, 2012, https://www.army.mil/article/85606/first_female_four_star_general_retires_from_army.

158   *"Over the last thirty-eight years, I have had the opportunity"*: ibid.

159   *"It was something that I felt I should do"*: "Dream Strong: Sgt. Sherri Jo Gallagher," GoArmy.com, YouTube,

https://www.youtube.com/watch?v=9VIaNVJy4XQ.

159   *"It was faster-paced, quick, reactive shooting"*: Brian Lepley, Michael Molinaro, and Alexandra Hemmerly-Brown, "Sgt. Sherri Gallagher Chosen as U.S. Army Soldier of the Year," Daily Bulletin, AccurateShooter.com, October 26, 2010, http://bulletin.accurateshooter.com/2010/10/sgt-sherri-gallagher-chosen-as-u-s-army-soldier-of-the-year/.

160   *"This course has proven"*: Mark Thompson, "Female Army Ranger Grads Are Among Nation's Top Soldiers, but Can't Fight," *Time*, Aug. 18, 2015, http://time.com/4002273/female-army-grads/.

161   *"I was thinking really"*: Brakkton Booker, "First Female Army Rangers Say They Thought of 'Future Generations of Women,'" The Two-Way: Breaking News from NPR, Aug. 20, 2015, https://www.npr.org/sections/thetwo-way/2015/08/20/433241833/first-female-army-rangers-say-they-thought-of-future-generations-of-women.

161   *"There was no pressure"*: Michelle Tan, "Congressman Wants Proof Standards Weren't Fudged for Female Ranger School Attendees," *Army Times*, Sept. 22, 2015, https://www.armytimes.com/news/pentagon-congress/2015/09/23/congressman-wants-proof-standards-weren-t-fudged-for-female-ranger-school-attendees/.

165   *"It's just something that happened"*: Rachel Martin, "Silver Star Recipient a Reluctant Hero," *Morning Edition*, NPR, Feb. 22, 2011, https://www.npr.org/2011/02/22/133847765/silver-star-recipient-a-reluctant-hero.

166   *"I wanted to do something"*: Thomas Gibbons-Neff, "The Marines Didn't Think Women Belonged in the Infantry. She's Proving Them Wrong." *New York Times*, Aug. 9, 2018.

167   *"I loved the idea of going out"*: Gretel C. Kovach, "Marine Woman Flies Blue Angels to New Heights," *San Diego Union-Tribune*, Oct. 1, 2015, http://www.sandiegouniontribune.com/military/sdut-blue-angels-female-pilot-katie-higgins-2015oct01-htmlstory.html.

168   *"I definitely appreciate the support from the American people"*: ibid.

168   *"He thanked me essentially for"*: ibid.

170   *"Women can not only be in the military"*: Melanie Stawicki Azam, "Super Heroine: Alumna Is One of Few Military Women to Earn a Distinguished Flying Cross for Heroism," *Lift*, Fall 2017, https://lift.erau.edu/super-heroine/.

171   *"[Horoho] has earned this extremely important leadership position"*: Rob McIlvaine, "Horoho Takes Oath as First Nurse, Female Surgeon General," U.S. Army, Dec. 8, 2011, https://www.army.mil/article/70556/horoho_takes_oath_as_first_nurse_female_surgeon_general.

172   *"We could not be more proud"*: J. Snyderman, "After 10 years, Pentagon First Responder Says America Stands Strong," Defense Visual Information Distribution Service, Sept. 9, 2011, https://www.dvidshub.net/news/76759/after-10-years-pentagon-first-responder-says-america-stands-strong.

173   *"representation of how far we have come"*: Dan Lamothe, "Adm. Michelle Howard Becomes First Four-Star Woman in Navy History, *Washington Post*, July 2, 2014, https://www.washingtonpost.com/news/checkpoint/wp/2014/07/01/adm-michelle-howard-becomes-first-four-star-woman-in-navy-history

/?utm_term=.2036d4c44515.

175　*"I didn't know it was possible"*: "A Four-Star Female Admiral Makes History for the Navy," *New York Times*, July 11, 2014, https://www.nytimes.com/2014/07/12/us/12admiral.html?mtrref=www.google.com&gwh=1F0E0A7BD40843115D21E17B05480057&gwt=pay&assetType=nyt_now.

175　*"I thought if I didn't have the courage"*: Scott Wyland, "US Navy's 1st Female 4-Star Admiral Set to Retire," *Stars and Stripes*, Sept. 26, 2017, https://www.stripes.com/news/us-navy-s-1st-female-4-star-admiral-set-to-retire-1.489556.

176　*"I hadn't realized what a big deal"*: "First Female Commanding Officer of a U.S. Navy Ship," Navy Life: The Official Blog of the U.S. Navy, Dec. 26, 2012, http://navylive.dodlive.mil/2012/12/26/first-female-commanding-officer-of-a-u-s-navy-warship/.

177　*"Once they opened the ships"*: "Equalize: Women Divers in the United States Navy—Darlene Iskra: Commander, U.S. Navy (retired)," All Hands: History and Heritage, http://www.navy.mil/ah_online/deptStory.asp?dep=8&issue=3&id=93275&page=5.

177　*"I knew I was the first (woman)"*: ibid.

177　*"All the men had ever seen women do"*: ibid.

177　*"The Navy changed my life"*: "Darlene Iskra," VFW: Veterans of Foreign Wars, https://www.vfw.org/advocacy/women-veterans/our-stories/darlene-iskra.

179　*"We heard shots and suddenly"*: "Essence Exclusive: Shoshana Johnson's Story," Essence.com, Dec. 16, 2009, https://www.essence.com/2004/02/13/essence-exclusive-shoshana-johnsons-stor.

180　*"I think I'm a stronger person"*: "Then & Now: Shoshana Johnson," CNN.com, June 19, 2005, http://www.cnn.com/2005/US/05/23/cnn25.tan.johnson/.

182　*"I don't try to emulate"*: Elaine Woo, "Kathleen McGrath, 50; 1st Woman to Command a U.S. Navy Warship," *Los Angeles Times*, Oct. 3, 2002, http://articles.latimes.com/2002/oct/03/local/me-mcgrath3.

183　*"I did flight training in a Cessna 172"*: Chuck Carlson, "Battle Creek Native Reaches Grand Heights in Air Force," *Coloradoan*, March 3, 2014, https://www.coloradoan.com/story/news/2014/03/04/battle-creek-native-reaches-grand-heights-in-air-force/5983661/.

183　*"That's when I fell in love"*: ibid.

184　*"I want to be a good listener"*: Master Sgt. Bob Haskell, "ANG Woman Wing Commander Doesn't See Herself as Pioneer," U.S. Department of Defense, March 18, 2004, http://archive.defense.gov/news/newsarticle.aspx?id=27044.

184　*"We really appreciate their service"*: Carlson, "Battle Creek Native."

185　*"I grew up as a kid"*: Marcella A. Hayes Ng: First African American Woman Pilot in the Armed Forces," Army Women's Foundation, https://www.awfdn.org/trailblazers/marcella-a-hayes-ng/.

186　*"Women were no longer separate"*: Charlotte Young, "Marcy Ng: America's First Black Woman Military Pilot," *MadameNoire*, January 18, 2012, http://madamenoire.com/129797/marcy-ng-americas-first-black-woman-military-pilot/.

189 *"We need to honor all the veterans"*: Diana Washington Valdez, "Battle Heroes of Fort Bliss Maintenance Company Remembered," *Stars and Stripes*, March 23, 2013, https://www.stripes.com/news/army
/battle-heroes-of-fort-bliss-maintenance-company-remembered-1.213200.

190 *"My father used to say"*: Brittany Carlson, U.S. Army, "Judge Shares Story at USALSA Asian-Pacific Heritage Observance," May 22, 2014, https://www.army.mil/article/126588/judge_shares_story_at_usalsa_asian
_pacific_heritage_observance.

191 *"I know what it is like to serve"*: "Opening Statement of Coral Wong Pietsch, Nominee for Judge of the
United States Court of Appeals for Veterans Claims," United States Senate Committee on Veteran's Affairs,
March 28, 2012, https://www.veterans.senate.gov/imo/media/doc/pietsch-3-28-12.pdf.

192 *"It is an honor"*: Gregg Birnbaum and Ryan Browne, "First Female Combatant Commander Takes
Charge," CNN Politics, May 13, 2016, https://www.cnn.com/2016/05/13/politics/first-woman-combatant
-commander-lori-robinson/index.html.

192 *"She was selected because"*: ibid.

193 *"I often say to people"*: Dan Lamothe, "Air Force Gen. Lori Robinson Becomes First Woman Ever to Lead
U.S. Combatant Command," *Washington Post*, May 13, 2016, https://www.washingtonpost.com/news
/checkpoint/wp/2016/05/13/air-force-gen-lori-robinson-becomes-first-woman-ever-to-lead-u-s
-combatant-command/?utm_term=.0107053927c4.

194 *"Why aren't you a Marine?"*: Deborah Knapp, "1st Latina Major General in Marines Is New CEO of Girl
Scouts of Southwest Texas," *Military Times*, Oct. 12, 2015, https://www.militarytimes.com/news/your
-military/2015/10/12/1st-latina-major-general-in-marines-is-new-ceo-of-girl-scouts-of-southwest-texas/.

194 *"It ignited in me"*: Eric Moreno, "Major General Angela Salinas; Military Leader Brings Passion for Service
to Girl Scouts of America," *San Antonio Magazine*, June 2016, http://www.sanantoniomag.com/June-2016
/Major-General-Angela-Salinas/.

195 *"It's a special breed of people"*: Tricia Schwennesen, "Women's Leadership Awards Keynote Speaker: Retired Maj. Gen. Angela Salinas," *San Antonio Business Journal*, Aug. 24, 2017, https://www.bizjournals.com
/sanantonio/news/2017/08/24/womens-leadership-awards-keynote-speaker-retired.html.

196 *"I remember thinking about"*: Don Markus, "Woman from Ellicott City a Coast Guard Pioneer," *Baltimore
Sun*, Nov. 30, 2009, http://articles.baltimoresun.com/2009-11-30/news/bal-md.ho.admiral30nov30_1
_cpast-guard-academy-navy.

197 *"I was the only female"*: Dan Chu, "She's No Party Animal, but When It Comes to Breaking the Ice, Sandra
Stosz Knows No Peer," *People*, April 8, 1991, http://people.com/archive/shes-no-party-animal-but-when-it
-comes-to-breaking-the-ice-sandra-stosz-knows-no-peer-vol-35-no-13/.

197 *"I don't see this so much"*: Craig Collins, "Interview: Rear Adm. Sandra L. Stosz, USCG," Defense Media
Network, Dec. 23, 2011, https://www.defensemedianetwork.com/stories/interview-rear-adm-sandra-l
-stosz-uscg/.

198 *"And it is"*: "Army Medicine's First African American Female Two-Star General," *Journal of the Student*

National Medical Association, May 8, 2013, http://jsnma.org/2013/05/army-medicines-first-african-american-female-two-star-general/.

198   *"I went from an orphan"*: Dana Bash, "How 3-Star General Nadja West Overcame Self-doubt," CNN Politics, June 16, 2017, https://www.cnn.com/2017/06/16/politics/nadja-west-badass-women-of-washington/index.html.

198   *"One characteristic that stands out"*: Adam Bryant, "Lt. Gen. Nadja Y. West on the Power of Empathy," *New York Times*, July 1, 2017, https://www.nytimes.com/2017/06/30/business/nadja-y-west-power-of-empathy.html?mtrref=www.google.com&gwh=F9538535B352D5BE5DA0C0F965210604&gwt=pay.

199   *"I couldn't wait to sign up"*: "Army Medicine's First African American Female Two-Star General," *Journal of the Student National Medical Association*.

199   *"If you told me"*: Bash, CNN Politics.

199   *"My parents taught me"*: *Journal of the Student National Medical Association*, May 8, 2013.

200   *"I think she's had an enormous impact"*: Linda Kramer, "Air Force Secretary Widnall Stepping Down," All Politics, CNN/Time, Oct.10, 1997, http://www.cnn.com/ALLPOLITICS/1997/10/10/widnall.kramer/.

201   *"We're not done"*: "Retiring 4-Star General Built Career on Hard Work, Positive Attitude," *Dayton Daily News*, May 12, 2015; https://www.mydaytondailynews.com/news/local-military/retiring-star-general-built-career-hard-work-positive-attitude/xJFYkKhHBZTJ1lUFCrpgPK/?source=ddn_skip_stub#49cb5019.3554830.735731.

202   *"learned and grown from every"*: ibid.

202   *"Never would have expected that I would"*: ibid.

204   *"It was like finally giving a team jersey"*: Tanya Biank, *Undaunted: The Real Story of America's Servicewomen in Today's Military* (New York: NAL Caliber, 2013), 4.

205   *"Aim High"*: "Words to Live by: 20 Top Military Mottos," Military 1, Oct. 30, 2014, https://www.military1.com/military-community/article/539431-words-to-live-by-20-top-us-military-mottos/.

BIBLIOGRAPHY

Abbott, Karen. *Liar, Temptress, Soldier, Spy: Four Women Undercover in the Civil War.* New York: Harper, 2014.

Allen, Thomas B. *Harriet Tubman, Secret Agent: How Daring Slaves and Free Blacks Spied for the Union During the Civil War.* Washington, DC: National Geographic Society, 2006.

Atwood, Kathryn J. *Courageous Women of the Vietnam War: Medics, Journalists, Survivors, and More.* Chicago, IL: Chicago Review Press, 2018.

——. *Women Heroes of World War II: The Pacific Theater: 15 Stories of Resistance, Rescue, Sabotage, and Survival.* Chicago, IL: Chicago Review Press, 2017.

——. *Women Heroes of World War II: 26 Stories of Espionage, Sabotage, Resistance, and Rescue.* Chicago, IL: Chicago Review Press, 2011.

Beyer, Kurt. *Grace Hopper and the Invention of the Information Age.* Cambridge, MA: MIT Press, 2012.

Blanton, DeAnne, and Lauren M. Cook. *They Fought Like Demons: Women Soldiers of the Civil War.* New York: Vintage, 2003. First published 2002 by Louisiana State University Press.

Bourke-White, Margaret. *Portrait of Myself.* New York: Simon & Schuster, 1963.

Bradford, Sarah H. *Scenes in the Life of Harriet Tubman.* Auburn, NY: W. J. Moses, 1869. https://archive.org/details/scenesinlifeofha1869brad.

Casey, Susan. *Women Heroes of the American Revolution: 20 Stories of Espionage, Sabotage, Defiance, and Rescue.* Chicago, IL: Chicago Review Press, 2015.

Cochran, Jacqueline, and Maryann Bucknum Brinley. *Jacqueline Cochran: An Autobiography.* New York: Bantam, 1987.

Colman, Penny. *Breaking the Chains: The Crusade of Dorothea Lynde Dix.* New York: ASJA Press, 2007. First published 1992 by Shoe Tree Press.

Earley, Charity Adams. *One Woman's Army: A Black Officer Remembers the WAC.* College Station: Texas A&M University Press, 1989.

Ebbert, Jean, and Marie-Beth Hall. *The First, the Few, the Forgotten: Navy and Marine Corps Women in World War I.* Annapolis, MD: Naval Institute Press, 2002.

Edmonds, Sarah Emma. *Memoirs of a Soldier, Nurse, and Spy: A Woman's Adventures in the Union Army.* DeKalb: Northern Illinois University Press, 1999.

Eggleston, Larry G. *Women in the Civil War: Extraordinary Stories of Soldiers, Spies, Nurses, Doctors, Crusaders, and Others.* Jefferson, NC: McFarland, 2003.

Eisner, Peter. *MacArthur's Spies: The Soldier, the Singer, and the Spymaster Who Defied the Japanese in World War II.* New York: Viking, 2017.

Farrell, Mary Cronk. *Pure Grit: How American World War II Nurses Survived Battle and Prison Camp in the Pacific.* New York: Abrams Books for Young Readers, 2014.

Fessler, Diane Burke. *No Time for Fear: Voices of American Military Nurses in World War II*. East Lansing: Michigan State University Press, 1997.

Godson, Susan H. *Serving Proudly: A History of Women in the U.S. Navy*. Annapolis, MD: Naval Institute Press, 2001.

Goldsmith, Bonnie Z. *Dr. Mary Edwards Walker: Civil War Soldier and Medal of Honor Recipient*. Edina, MN: ABDO Publishing, 2010.

Hancock, Joy Bright. *Lady in the Navy: A Personal Reminiscence*. Annapolis, MD: Bluejacket Books, 2002. First published 1972 by Naval Institute Press.

Harness, Cheryl. *Mary Walker Wears the Pants: The True Story of the Doctor, Reformer, and Civil War Hero*. Chicago, IL: Albert Whitman, 2013.

Johnson, Shoshana, with M. L. Doyle. *I'm Still Standing: From Captive U.S. Soldier to Free Citizen—My Journey Home*. New York: Simon & Schuster, 2010.

Joinson, Carla. *Civil War Doctor: The Story of Mary Walker*. Greensboro, NC: Morgan Reynolds, 2007.

Jones, Carrie. *Sarah Emma Edmonds Was a Great Pretender: The True Story of a Civil War Spy*. Minneapolis, MN: Carolrhoda Books, 2011.

Klass, Sheila Solomon. *Soldier's Secret: The Story of Deborah Sampson*. New York: Henry Holt Books for Young Readers, 2009.

Muckenhoupt, Meg. *Dorothea Dix: Advocate for Mental Health Care*. New York: Oxford University Press, 2003.

Norman, Elizabeth M. *We Band of Angels: The Untold Story of the American Women Trapped on Bataan*. New York: Random House Trade Paperbacks, 2013. First published 1999 by Random House.

Oertel, Kristen T. *Harriet Tubman: Slavery, the Civil War, and Civil Rights in the Nineteenth Century*. New York: Routledge, 2016.

Pelleschi, Andrea. *Mathematician and Computer Scientist Grace Hopper*. Minneapolis, MN: Lerner Classroom, 2016.

Rich, Doris L. *Jackie Cochran: Pilot in the Fastest Lane*. Gainesville: University Press of Florida, 2010. First published 2007 by University Press of Florida.

Shiels, Damian. *The Irish in the American Civil War*. Mt. Pleasant, SC: History Press/Arcadia Publishing, 2014.

Smith-Daugherty, Rhonda. *Jacqueline Cochran: Biography of a Pioneer Aviator*. Jefferson, NC: McFarland, 2012.

Wakeman, Sarah Rosetta. *An Uncommon Soldier: The Civil War Letters of Sarah Rosetta Wakeman, alias, Pvt. Lyons Wakeman, 153rd Regiment, New York State Volunteers, 1862–1864*. Edited by Lauren Cook Burgess. New York: Oxford University Press, 1995. First published 1994 by Minerva Center.

Walker, Dale L. *Mary Edwards Walker: Above and Beyond*. New York: Forge Books, 2005.

Wallmark, Laurie. *Grace Hopper: Queen of Computer Code*. New York: Sterling Children's Books, 2017.

Winegarten, Debra L. *Oveta Culp Hobby: Colonel, Cabinet Member, Philanthropist*. Austin: University of Texas Press, 2014.

Young, Alfred F. *Masquerade: The Life and Times of Deborah Sampson, Continental Soldier*. New York: Vintage Books, 2005. First published 2004 by Alfred A. Knopf.

INDEX